...RY HERE and the map at the back of the book rep-
...the situation in each area as of the first time the
...come upon it. Assuming the players do nothing
...them, the following events will occur (and if they
...st the 24th, they will see them recur again):

...(New Moon) **DAY OF THE PURIFIER:** The Amazon
...ribes wear whalebone masks in observance
...of Fastelavn. Ratatoskr sees his shadow.

...(Waxing Crescent Moon) Mad Maggot Queen
...Rindr finds the rat called Ribboned Jenny.
...Bartering for her freedom with the mad queen,
...enny reveals that she knows Prince Nygnengeth
...of Nornrik is hunting in the Devoured Land.

...(Waxing Crescent Moon) Sam the Moth and
...Garvik Nerves of the Arsonists have an
...argument. After two days of searching, Nerves
...wants to find the secret entrance to the Dim
...Fortress, Sam wants easier prey. Sam leaves.

...(Waxing Crescent Moon) Stryx the owl
...sees Ratatoskr emerge from a secret
...entrance to the Dim Fortress, bringing
...gossip to the trolls of Lachrymose Peak.

...(Waxing Crescent Moon) Sam the Moth is captured
...by the Peak trolls while trying to steal their gold.

...(Waxing Crescent Moon) Frostbitten Moons
...have a large but indecisive battle with the
...Ulvenbrigad. The Moons begin to wonder
...why the Ulvenbrigad are so far north.

...(First Quarter Moon) Sam escapes.

...(Waxing Gibbous Moon) Sam sees the
...witch Dread's retinue, disguised as Prince
...Nygnengeth's, consulting the trolls.

...(Waxing Gibbous Moon) The owl Stryx
...meets up with Tormentor, familiar of
...the witch called Frost, tells her about the
...secret entrance to the Dim Fortress.

...(Waxing Gibbous Moon) Garvik Nerves offers a
...deal to Black Sky, Nerves will give them half the
...treasure from the Dim Fortress if they protect
...the Arsonists until they find an entrance.

...(Waxing Gibbous Moon) Maggot Sisters
...capture Sam who offers to lead the Sisters to
...the "Prince" in exchange for her freedom...

...a Maggot Sister and discover Rindr's plan.

16TH (Waning Gibbous Moon) The Thirteen
battle a werewolf, take casualties.

17TH (Waning Gibbous Moon) A group of the
Ulvenbrigad capture some of the remaining
Thirteen, including Malicia Orgen.

18TH (Waning Gibbous Moon) The Frostbitten
Moons defeat the main force of the
Ulvenbrigad. The captured Thirteen flee.

19TH (Waning Gibbous Moon) The Frostbitten Moo...
search for and round up the fleeing Thirteen...

20TH (Waning Gibbous Moon) The Thirteen
reveal to the Moons that they've learned
of the Maggot Sisters' plans to aid the
witches entering the Dim Fortress.

21ST (Waning Gibbous Moon) A war party of
the Frostbitten Moons attacks and is
defeated by the Maggot Sisterhood,
however, a Cold Banner assassin manages
to infiltrate the Sisterhood's ranks.

22ND (Third Quarter Moon) Rindr and the three
witches—Thorn, Frost, and Dread—meet a...
Gutgloaming Lake (G8). Frost agrees to lead...
them to the entrance to the Dim Fortress,
which she has learned about from Torment...

23RD (Waning Crescent Moon) The witches and a h...
of Maggots head north toward the mounta...

24TH (Waning Crescent Moon) The festival of
Dragobete. Late that night, the host
approaches the Arsonists' camp. Cold Bann...
assassin slays Queen Rindr, the Arsonists
take advantage of the disarray to attack, th...
witches summon Stryx's parliament of owl...
to defend them from the crows. The witche...
eventually drive off the Arsonists but by
then it's too late to enter the mountain...

ﬀrostbitten &ﬃutilated

Writing and art by Zak Smith
Editing by Joshua Blackketter
Design by Luka Rejec

LFP0047
Text and Art ©2018 Zak Smith
Issued under exclusive license to:

LAMENTATIONS
of the
FLAME PRINCESS

www.lotfp.com
ISBN Print: 978-952-7238-02-8
ISBN PDF: 978-952-7238-03-5
Printed in Finland by Otava Book Printing, Ltd.
First Printing: 5000 copies
Lamentations of the Flame Princess
is a registered trademark owned
by James Edward Raggi IV

Dedication

ON PAGE 27 OF THE FIRST D&D book's first
volume there appears an illustration of
two creatures—"Beautiful Witch" (left) and
"Amazon" (right)—drawn by one Cookie
Corey. They are, true to that volume's
subtitle ("Men & Magic"), not described
anywhere in the text. The image therefore
represents not only the first work done
by a woman in RPGs and the first female
characters published in an RPG but also
the first hack of an RPG. So: this one is for
Cookie Corey.

Zak Smith, 2017

Note on the appropriation of traditional Nordic cultures

THIS BOOK WOEFULLY misrepresents Norse culture. I mean—probably it does, it has monsters I made up in it—I don't know I'm Jewish. Anyway, enjoy.

"Outside in the cold night the wind moaned and died down, like an idiot in an icy black pit."
                                    -Richard Wright, *Native Son*

Table of Contents

THE GODS FROZE SOUNDS—making words—and set the creatures working, to cut languages from the ice. A troll was set to grinding and was resentful, despising all improvement. The grinding troll worked, but poisoned twenty-one words in every tongue—so they would work a mischief in the mouths of men and bring them to ruin.

The She-Goat knew what the gods did not, and sought to thwart the grinding-troll. She went to the Place of the Ears of Women and whis-pered into one in each one hundred thousand right ears, saying "Twenty-one words are poison, but I know not which. Take no sense from the tongues of men. Go now uncorrupted."

When women were assembled, one in one hundred thousand were given these ears and this mark—that they would be made weary by the speech of men, and avoid it. They dwell now alone in the long cold crawling—heeding no-one.

How to use this book

THIS BOOK BASICALLY has three parts:

† tools and toys to help you make
  adventures featuring extremely metal
  things like warrior women, frost
  giants, and apocalyptic monsters
† a specific setting (The Devoured Land)
  with specific places in it and maps and
  specific people and monsters that want
  specific stuff that you can use if you want
† a calendar of events that begins when
  the party arrives in The Devoured Land
  and which will move forward if the
  party doesn't do anything about them

...you should be able to use all-, most-, or
some of these parts without anything bad
happening. However, I don't recommend using
none of them—I mean I don't know your situation personally but probably if you do that your
game will suck and you'll die weeping on a pile
of rags, universally despised.

Some advice for the Referee

GET THE RIGHT MUSIC. Then, before you run the game, create the quietest, darkest situation you can.

Sit without moving, with your finger resting lightly on the music button—whichever it is: play, enter, the click, the rightward arrow.

Think of an empty landscape—only the drag of a flatlining horizon separates white sky from white earth. There is one thing: a lone thin black tree, bare, reaching like a python. It is a distant but clear shape.

Imagine it. Imagine it and hear your own breath. In and then out again. Touch the button.

There's a second silhouette that emerges beneath and it is the silhouette of the worst person you know. Imagine, summon and indulge real emotion—a person for whom you feel (not *believe you should feel*—but **feel**) total enmity, total opposition—and if you subscribe to a philosophy whereby these emotions are to be suppressed, put away that philosophy now. It is given to you to know that for this foe there is no hope of reform and no other life where punishment will be administered. They stand, seeing you as you see them.

In the sound and the dark, totally experience your hatred of them, the heat of it, the hatred of their face, their many ways, their words. Give it some time there. Know that you are human, that to despise is human and what is common to your kind is natural. It is of nature. Knowing this hate, knowing this unity, know this too: this is how the landscape feels about your players' characters. This is it how it views their trespass, the formlessness of the way they slather themselves across itself. Their steps set the entire cold world to seething. It needs, and seeks, their downfall. By force and by calculation. By means known and as yet unknown. It will devise methods. This is nature: it will innovate to extend the reach of its hate.

Turn the light back on, your players are coming—but look at your hand and make a claw, then from the claw make a fist. Hold what you have learned there in that fist. Keep it away—these are, after all, your friends. It is important to have allies in this life and you owe them all you can spare—you owe them all the warmth in the world. Give them snacks—give them whatever will please them most, tell them jokes. Fortify them against less merciful futures.

But when you are at play and must play the cold world described in this book and its manifestations, you now know its heart. You hold it quietly in one hand, and may consult it.

Recommended

Read these:

THE ARTHUR GILCHRIST BRODEUR 1916 translation of the *Gylfaginning* in Snorri Sturlson's *Younger Edda* is a good place to start—that's where you can read about how they made the sky out of a rime-giant's skull and whatnot. The rest of the *Eddas* are recommended by anyone who writes an RPG book with viking stuff in it.

Fritz Leiber's *The Snow Women* is the best Fafhrd and Grey Mouser short story and one of the best short stories period and one of the best things period. So read it even if you don't ever play a game again.

Walt Simonson's *Thor* issues 337-367 and 380, the all-full-page-art issue where Thor fights the Midgard Serpent.

Mallory Ortberg's *Early Signs of Pregnancy*.

Maybe this:

I HAVE VERY DIM memories of being read Steven Bauer's novel *Satyrday* as a child and it probably influenced my treatment of animals here. I almost gave the moon stats.

Listen to this:

FOR TRUE NORWEGIAN Black Metal, **Immortal** is my favorite, and *"All Shall Fall"* is the maximum dose. For the Amazons themselves the soundtrack is **Thorr's Hammer**, **Jex Thoth**, **Kylesa**, and **13** (the 13 that did *"Whore"* *"Hollow"* and *"Writhe"*). **Svartsinn** is good to have on in dungeons and **Wolves in the Throne Room** is good everywhere else.

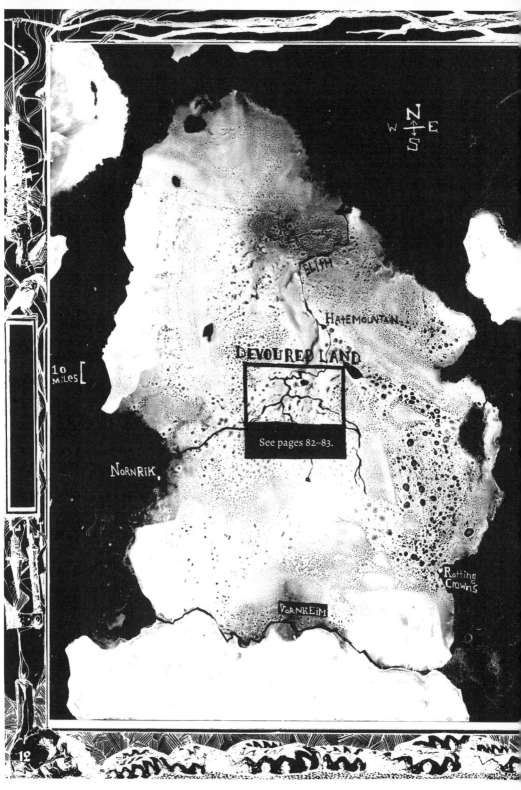

DEVOURED LAND

See pages 82–83.

SLiFM

HateMountain

NoRNRiK

Rotting Crowns

VORNHEiM

10 miles

12

Adventures in the Devoured Land

SOMETIMES THE SNOW will not stop. Under its particled screen like layers of veil that would make of the world a bride to an unknown, vast and unseen groom all civilization is wondering from its hearths and stone corners: What is to be done about the women? They spit and rage, they drown the taxmen, they hack the bellies of snakes and eat what they find, they abort babies and squeeze their milk into the bellies of troll-cats, they dwell apart among the wide white peaks, raiding, scheming, speaking to animals, willful and without trade or diplomatic discourse—the witch-women and amazons. They dominate and divide the Devoured Land. Who can see this ending well?

Why might you travel to the Devoured Land—a death-place where mountains, ice-crowned, claw at the sky and nothing is ordinary?

Gold

SOMETHING PLUNDERS those caravans that never come back. Some say there are greedy frost giants with great hoards, but some say this is a lie told by cowards to disguise having fled frightened from armed women.

Anarchy

THE LAWLESS DEVOURED LAND is a place for a party to hide if they are fugitives and a place for them to scour if they are in pursuit of one.

Wisdom

IT MAY BE THE OLDEST place in the world. Some claim the Darkthrone of Ovv, the first king, lies somewhere deep in the mountains' belly. Some say the worst three witches live in the Devoured Land, and that they will inculcate the end of all things. There is magic here not seen since night first divided from day.

Embryoctony

MIDWIVES IN EVERY CITY whisper that the Amazons know the secrets to safely unseat a child before it can escape a womb to inhale and swallow a soul, and that the herbs of Mount Hellebor make the procedure painless. Desperate women of good families have been known to disguise themselves and quietly hire bands of armed escorts to take them north, while claiming to be visiting aunts in warm climes.

Getting there

YOU ARE NOT YET in the Devoured Land, where there are no men alive and the world is ripped away from itself. You will be soon. The unexplored wastes are large, do what you like with them. Outside the map you will be given, with 64 areas partially filled in for you, there are only four things to remember: the sea—from which flows the River Slith, the Hatemountain—where the frost giants live, and two outposts of what men do, and women often do not, call "civilization". They are:

Nornrik

THIS IS A CITY, with a castle and lords and everything. Sophisticated, brittle, mannered. As large as you're comfortable making it. If you prefer a historical city, you can use Trondheim, which was the Norwegian capital during the Viking era and is eminently Googleable.

Rottingkroner

THE CLOSEST HARBOR to the Devoured Land, also known as Rotting Crowns—named for the enfolding shape of the abraded rock formations comprising the surrounding fjord. Merchants and seaman come to be tattooed, regaled with rumor, murdered, and inveigled into any other grotty seaport cliché your campaign requires.

ALTHOUGH THIS module is set in the same world as my book *Vornheim: The Complete City Kit*, it can as easily be set in a semi-historical Norway. Just remember Norway has no East coast, so its equivalent of Rottingkroner would be somewhere to the west of the Devoured Land map provided.

We're going to the Devoured Land now, which will first be described by describing who lives there in alphabetical order. This is surprisingly convenient: It starts with Amazons, Animals, and Avalanches, and finishes with Witches and Wolves and Worms.

Inhabitants

THE DEVOURED LAND IS DISTANT, unfathomed. They say the cleft peaks are the uneaten half left torn when the first Cannibal God bit the world. Things there are as things were in the day before all days, when all that is now knew a common tongue and a young, smoother moon hung pearl-like in a black bed gestating the unborn stars.

The ice is clearer, the wind sharper, every sound echoes, and all time unravels with a clear and open order. The ancient tolerance with which each con-temporary thing regards and gnaws at the thing adjacent in our sensical and passive-aggressive

explicit. The shadow falls across the rock, and the rock despises that. The oldest witch is here, the proudest stag, the most vicious wolf, the fattest hog and most lustful goat, the most avid crow, the most resentful of rats, and worms so lazy they have been here since "here" began.

There are trees that grew in first rain, and horses that have never known a rider, stones cut by the hand of the first women and recut by thousands after, parasites grown from the guts of the first men, there are fortresses buried since the first bat-tle. It's said time started and will end in this place.

INHABITANTS

AMAZONS

WHO SAYS THIS? The Amazons. But then: they will say anything. To you, anyway. I know because you can read this and I wrote it and I wrote it in a language of cities and so if you can read it you are not one of them. So they will lie to you. Or tell you the truth. Whichever is more likely to frighten you away. If their knives, their war animals, their bacchanals, their cultured exotoxins, their enmity, cuisine, enigmatic gods, complex obstetrics, and internecine warfare have not frightened you first.

These are the daughters of the she-goat and they have chosen another path.

Their diet is meat mixed with things found while looking for meat, every craft they possess is taught after having learned the lessons of axes, bonebreaking, and the taking of blood. Amazons that are neither hunters nor reavers nor witches are called children—they have stats as ordinary humans and will bite for d4 damage.

These are a few of their tribes.

the Frostbitten Moons

Typical Frostbitten Moon

HD 3 **HP** 15 **SPEED** 120'
ARMOR 16 (leather armor + high Dex)
MORALE 10

ATTACK
† *Longbow*: +5 to hit d6hp.
† *Throwing axe*: +5 to hit d6+1hp.
† *Great axe*: +5 to hit d10+1hp.
† *Poisoned touch*: +5 to hit (touch attack) save vs Poison each round until a save is made, taking 2hp per failed save.

DEFENSE
† Anyone touching a Moon must save vs *Poison* each round until a save is made, taking 2hp per failed save.

SPECIAL
† *Bushcraft*: 3 in 6.

THE AMAZONS OF THE FROSTBITTEN MOON are the major human presence in the area surrounding Mount Hellebor. They are known by the patterns of yellow pigment that stain their skins, made from the venom of a strain of cross adder—to which continual contact and/or low necromancy provides them a contact immunity. They wear jewelry cast from the frozen tears of their foes.

Their current concern is the infiltration of their territory by the Maggot Sisterhood and the Ulvenbrigad.

Cold Banner

THE COLD BANNER is a secret society within the Frostbitten Moon tribe that carries out targeted assassinations. Each member wears a mask of painted bone. Their esoteric ceremonies are more disturbing than any ritual conceived in the civilized world.

Typical Cold Banner Assassin

HD 5 **HP** 25 **SPEED** 120'
ARMOR 16 (leather armor + high Dex)
MORALE 11
ATTACK

† **Poisoned longbow**: +7 to hit d6hp and save vs Poison or be Slowed as the spell for 10 rounds and take d12 damage.

† **Poisoned dagger**: +7 to hit d4+1hp and save vs Poison or be Slowed as the spell for 10 rounds and take d12 damage.

† **Poisoned touch**: +7 to hit, save vs Poison each round until a save is made, taking 2hp per failed save.

† *Sneak attack only*: +9 to hit, any of the above does *x3 wound damage* plus normal poison damage.

DEFENSE

† Anyone touching a Cold Banner assassin (when they are not in disguise) must save vs **Poison** each round until a save is made, taking 2hp per failed save.

SPECIAL

† **Climb**: 4 in 6.
† **Stealth**: 4 in 6.
† **Bushcraft**: 3 in 6.

Jex Amon

JEX AMON IS THE CURRENTLY elected warmistress of the Frostbitten Moons, her nails are long and poisonous. Guarded by elk-hunting **dogs named Taunter and Taker**, she also sleeps on **a bed of black snakes** which she claims are trained. They aren't really but since she's immune to their venom and you aren't, it kind of doesn't matter. Their leader is named **Sermon** and, aside from occasionally being thrown at people during raids, he leads a pampered life, about which he should not, and cannot, complain.

HD 8 **HP** 50 **SPEED** 120'

ARMOR 16 (leather armor + high Dex)

MORALE 11

ATTACKS (2 attacks per round)

† **Poisoned claw**: +10 to hit d6hp+2hp and save vs Poison or be Slowed as the spell for 10 rounds and take d12 damage.

† **Poisoned touch**: +10 to hit and save vs Poison or be Slowed as the spell for 10 rounds and take d12 damage.

† Throw a **tangle of snakes**: +10 to hit or you're in melee with d4+1 snakes.

DEFENSE

† Anyone touching Jex Amon must save vs Poison or be **Slowed** as the spell for 10 rounds and take d12 damage.

SPECIAL

† **Bushcraft**: 3 in 6.

Taunter and Taker (dogs)

HD 3 **HP** 15 **SPEED** 130'

ARMOR 14

MORALE 11

ATTACK

† **Bite**: +3 to hit 2d4+1hp.

Sermon and other serpents

HD 1 **HP** 5 **SPEED** 90'

ARMOR 14 **MORALE** 6

ATTACK

† **Bite**: +2 to hit d4hp and save vs Poison each round until a save is made, taking 2hp per failed save. If any saves are failed the affected body part will swell grotesquely and the character will take 5hp every morning until it is treated.

SPECIAL

† Sermon's skin, if read (see Serpents, pg 62), has a **list of places** in the Devoured Land where one can sleep on the 4th day of each week and meet no random encounters.

THE MAGGOT SISTERS are burners of churches, slovenly and bold, and notable for both the trained warpigs that serve them and the intricate record of slain foes tattooed on their bodies. By decree of their mad queen, **Rindr**, they strike first at Clerics, nuns, and members of holy orders, ignoring everything to bring them down. Her other eccentric edicts include a policy of stealing or burning wizard spell books and beheading enemies as soon as they fall, mid-battle, rather than leaving the unconscious to attack nearby allies. If a Maggot Sister kills you, she makes sure she kills you.

Typical Maggot Sister

HD 3 **HP** 15 **SPEED** 120'
ARMOR 16 (leather armor + high Dex)
MORALE 10
ATTACK

† *Longbow*: +5 to hit d6hp (+d4hp fire damage if there is time to prepare a fire arrow).
† *Net*: +5 to hit (touch attack) (Getting out of a net in the middle of combat requires a successful Sleight of Hand roll, doing 6 points of damage to the net, or two characters taking their whole action.).
† *Throwing axe*: +5 to hit d6+1hp.
† *Bastard sword*: +5 to hit d8+1hp.

SPECIAL

† Maggot Sisters employ *caltrops* (Dex check or take d4 damage and move at half speed) and flaming arrows if there is time to prepare.
† *Bushcraft*: 3 in 6.

Warpigs

HD 2 **HP** 10 **SPEED** 120'
ARMOR 14
MORALE 10
ATTACK

† *Bite*: +2 to hit 2d4hp.

the Maggot

Rindr

THE MAD QUEEN is known for her appetites, as well as her obsession with hidden knowledge. She has led her tribe into the territory of the Frostbitten Moons in search of the entrance to the fabled Dim Fortress, from which she hopes to liberate the ancient wyrm, **Nidhoggr**, for reasons unknown.

HD 8 **HP** 50 **SPEED** 120'

ARMOR 16 (leather armor + high Dex)

MORALE 11

ATTACKS (2 attacks per round)

† **Sickle on a chain**: +10 to hit—
   if the attack succeeds,
   the target is entangled
   and takes d8+2hp.

† **Great sword**: +10 to hit d10+2hp.

DEFENSE

† Rindr's thoughts are so disordered,
   she is **immune to mental attack**,
   including *Charm*, *ESP*, etc.

SPECIAL

† **Bushcraft**: 3 in 6.

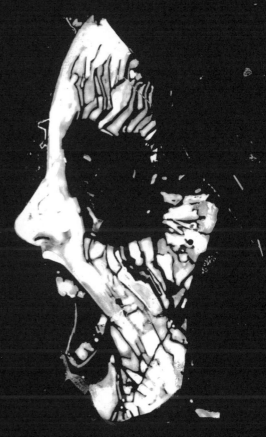

Sisterhood

the Thirteen

By far the least organized and most opportunistic of the Amazon clans in the Devoured Land, The Thirteen number only twenty-five. More a gang than a clan, they used to number thirteen—but when **Malicia Orgen** found a way to synthesize a powerful hallucinogenic powder from the scatter-rag lichen, she was made leader—and membership nearly doubled.

They are currently spying on the Maggot Sisterhood, whose presence near Mount Hellebor is both provocative and mysterious.

Typical Thirteen Sister

HD 3 **HP** 15 **Speed** 120'
Armor 16 (leather armor + high Dex)
Morale 9

Attack
† **Longbow**: +5 to hit d6hp.
† **Throwing axe**: +5 to hit d6+1hp.
† **Bastard sword**: +5 to hit d8+1hp.
† Throw bag of **Witherbound powder,** +5 to hit (touch attack) the target must save vs Poison—if failed, see *New Substances* section (pg 118) for effects.
   Range: 10', radius 5'.

Special
† **Stealth**: 3 in 6.
† **Sleight of hand**: 3 in 6.
† **Bushcraft**: 3 in 6.

Malicia Orgen

IT IS RUMORED THAT Orgen has eight eyes scattered across her body. It is certain she has one on her left palm, and an extensively informed curiosity about psychoactive plant life and the uses to which it can be put.

HD 8 **HP** 50 **SPEED** 120'

ARMOR 16 (leather armor + high Dex)

MORALE 9

ATTACK

† **Bite**: +10 to hit d4hp.

† **Throwing axe**: +10 to hit d6+1hp.

† **Great axe**: +10 to hit d10+1hp.

† Throw bag of **Witherbound powder**: +10 to hit (touch attack) the target must save vs Poison—if failed, see *New Substances* section (pg 118) for effects. Range: 10', radius 5'.

† Throw bag of **Flint powder**: 10' radius. Everyone save vs Poison. The targets who fail their saves take d6hp each round and can't see. Blindness persists until washed for one round in clean water and damage happens until the target spends a round vomiting.

SPECIAL

† Malicia can **see through her left palm** (at least) if it ever comes up.

† **Stealth**: 4 in 6.

† **Sleight of hand**: 3 in 6.

† **Bushcraft**: 3 in 6.

the Ulvenbrigad

COMPARED TO THE POISONOUS Frostbitten Moons and the Cleric-mobbing, decapitating Maggot Sisters, military historians and ethnographers might be tempted to consider the Ulvenbrigad the least dangerous of the major factions of Amazon in the Devoured Land if only it weren't for the trained wolves. And the necromancy. Any party of Ulvenbrigad will include at least one spellcaster and at least one wolf. In deference to Belphegor, Master of Beasts, and in exchange for concord with his creatures, the first attempted attack of any Ulvenbrigad sister will always be a bite. They are ruled by *Kylesamara* and *Marakylesa*, the lychewives, in consultation with the sacred bastard known as *Choard*.

They are currently pushing north into the territory of the Frostbitten Moons, hoping to take advantage of the chaos caused by whatever the Maggot Sisterhood has planned. They treat werewolves (like the one in location F5) like minor gods.

Typical Ulvenbrigad

HD 3 **HP** 15 **Speed** 120'
Armor 16 (leather armor + high Dex)
Morale 10
Attack
† **Bite**: +5 to hit d4hp.
† **Throwing axe**: +5 to hit d6+1hp.
† **Great axe**: +5 to hit d10+1hp.

Ulvenbrigad Wolves

HD 3 **HP** 15 **Speed** 120'
Armor 14
Morale 10 (Wolves never check morale until at least one foe is dead.)
Attack
† **Bite**: +3 to hit 2d4+1hp.
Special
† Anyone seeing a wolf must **drink a toast** to it the following night—or more will come.
† **Bushcraft**: 3 in 6.

Typical Ulvenbrigad Witch

HD 2 **HP** 10 **Speed** 120'
Armor 14
Morale 9
Attack
† **Bite**: +3 to hit d4hp.
† **Throwing axe**: +3 to hit d6+1hp.
† **Knife**: +3 to hit d4hp.
† **Spells** (2/day each) (these versions of these spells are deliverable only via bite or cursed knifepoint): *Chain of Skin* (see Spells), *Confusion, Command, Hold Person.*
Special
† The Ulvenbrigad witches have a wide variety of **other spells** available, these are just the ones they'll most typically use in a fight.
† **Language of Scales**: All Witches can read the skins of serpents.
† **Bushcraft**: 3 in 6.

Kylesamara & Maramylesa

WHEN A POWERFUL WITCH WISHES to extend her life beyond its natural span, she calls for two things: an immaculate, unwilling Cleric and a bone saw. Witch and virgin are divided down the middle and the halves are fused to their mismatched twins with baleful arts and catgut. This produces two lychewives—one lyche-sinister, one lyche-dexter.

Kylesa was the witch, and Mara the virgin. The Mara halves typically do nothing or scream and beg for death—being totally physically subservient to their Kylesa halves, who have led the Ulvenbrigad for 400 years.

Kylesamara

HD 12 **HP** 60 Kylesa half /60 Mara half **Speed** 120'
Armor 14
Morale 9
Attacks (2 attacks per round)

† **Desiccating touch**: +8 to hit 3d6hp.
† **Drain a level** from a helpless victim (save vs Magic allowed).
† Eerily **divided voice** can *Cause Fear* as the spell (counts as an action).
† **Spells** as 12th lvl Cleric and 12th lvl Magic-User. A typical selection includes 2 each of: *Paranoia, Web of Thorns, Death Spell, Command, Suggestion, Howl of the Moon, Forget.*

Defense

† The Mara half grants the lychewives **immunity to Cleric spells** of her god—Vorn, Odin, Jesus, or whatever the most popular local god is.
† The Kylesa halves are **undead** and so are immune to any magic that only affects the living. The Mara halves are not.
† **Damage** taken by the Kylesa halves **is split** with the Mara halves unless it only affects the undead.

Special

† The Mara halves of the lychewives are innocent and beloved by their gods. If they die in their unhallowed condition, all responsible (gods tend to interpret responsibility broadly) parties will be **unable to level up** until completing a quest of the god's choice (entering the Dim Fortress and destroying Nidhoggr is a typical one). The only way to avoid this fate is to separate the Kylesa from the halves Mara halves with a knife washed in holy water before the Mara half reaches ohp, consecrate the Mara halves, and give them a proper burial.
† **Language of Scales**: All Witches can read the skins of serpents.
† **Bushcraft**: 3 in 6.

Marakylesa

HD 12 **HP** 60 each half **Speed** 120'
Armor 14
Morale 9
Attacks (2 attacks per round)

† **Paralyzing touch**: +8 to hit, save vs Paralysis each round, effect lasts until a save is made.
† **Drain a level** from a helpless victim (save vs Magic allowed).
† Eerily **divided voice** can *Cause Fear* as the spell (counts as an action).
† **Spells** as 12th lvl Cleric and 12th lvl Magic-User. A typical selection includes: *Death Spell, Command, Suggestion, Howl of the Moon, Forget.*

Defense and Special (as Kylesamara)

Choard

THE SACRED BASTARD is a wallowing malformed quarter-dead thing fathered on Kylesamara by a drunken king some 80 years ago. Its thrashings and inchoate utterances are interpreted as portents by the lychewives. Maybe they are?

HD 1 **HP** 1 **Speed** 30'
Armor 10
Morale 3

ANJMALS in General

"Four."

"Five! I go first..."

"Bring it."

"So the wolves charge from both sides toward the middle of the column and attack Hellhammer."

"Wait, all of them?"

"Yes, all of them. That's...five hits for...22 point of damage..."

"Why are they all attacking me?"

"That's a good question. Try a Bushcraft roll..."

"I can't, I'm dead."

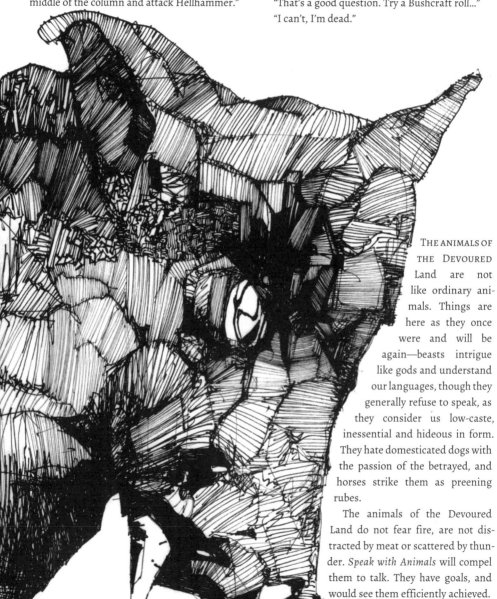

THE ANIMALS OF THE DEVOURED Land are not like ordinary animals. Things are here as they once were and will be again—beasts intrigue like gods and understand our languages, though they generally refuse to speak, as they consider us low-caste, inessential and hideous in form. They hate domesticated dogs with the passion of the betrayed, and horses strike them as preening rubes.

The animals of the Devoured Land do not fear fire, are not distracted by meat or scattered by thunder. *Speak with Animals* will compel them to talk. They have goals, and would see them efficiently achieved.

Arctic Foxes

THE ARCTIC FOX is not so much fond of strife as solitude—but it comes to the same thing. It attempts to lead groups of hostile apex megafauna (adventuring parties very much included) toward each other, in the hope that the subsequent clash will result in less of either or, preferably, both. It is not above making off with small items or leaving false trails to lead hunters toward each other and snickering in the shrubbery when they meet.

HD 1 **HP** 5 **SPEED** 180'
ARMOR 15 (high Dex)
MORALE 5
ATTACK
†   *Bite*: +3 to hit d4hp.
SPECIAL
†   *Stealth*: 5 in 6.
†   *Sleight of hand* (pickpocket): 4 in 6.

ARSONISTS

THE ARSONISTS ARE A SMALL BAND of adventurers from abroad—fond of experience, gold, and setting things alight.

Garvik Nerves

A BENT WIZARD, wiry and petulant, xenophobic—seeks the secret of the Dim Fortress with a charmless obsessiveness.

HD 7 **HP** 21 **SPEED** 120'

ARMOR 10

MORALE 8

ATTACK

† **Dagger**: +1 to hit d4hp.

† **Crossbow**: +2 to hit d6hp.

† Typical **spells** prepared: *Spider Climb, Feather Fall, Detect Magic, Web* (x3), *Invisibility 10' Radius, Haste, Dimension Door*

Samantha the Moth

A LONG-HAIRED ASSASSIN of Nornrik—resourceful, vain, a collector of obscure armaments.

HD 7 **HP** 15 **SPEED** 120'

ARMOR 17

MORALE 10

ATTACK

† **Bohemian ear-spoon** (pole arm): +9 d8+2hp.

† **Sword-breaker** (slotted short sword): +9 to hit d6hp. If used to parry, a successful parry (a miss that would've hit without the +4 Armor bonus) means the wielder breaks the enemy's sword if they win initiative the next round and succeed in a Str check.

† **Elk-head shield**: +9 to hit d6hp from horns

† **Poison-bulb arrow longbow**: +9 to hit d4hp plus save vs Poison or sleep until you take half your remaining hp worth of damage.

† **Spiky ball** (thrown): +9 to hit d8+2hp (baseball sized).

SPECIAL

† **Stealth**: 4 in 6.

Minnthic Phythit

A RELENTLESS BUT RELENTLESSLY PRAGMATIC thief of northern continental extraction. Carries caltrops, marbles, and lubricant everywhere. Claims to have stolen a barony.

HD 7 **HP** 20 **SPEED** 120'

ARMOR 14

MORALE 7

ATTACK

† **Crossbow**: +1 to hit d6hp.

† **Longsword**: +1 to hit d8hp.

† Also carries **caltrops**, **marbles**, **lard**, 5 **jars of oil**, **beartrap** (save vs Device or 2d6hp).

† **Sneak attack** x6.

SPECIAL

† **Stealth**: 5 in 6.

† **Climb**: 5 in 6.

† **Search**: 4 in 6.

Mormit Mythe

CARTOGRAPHER AND LITHOGRAPHER. A ferocious woman—one hand a heavy claw.

HD 6 **HP** 30 **SPEED** 120'

ARMOR 16

MORALE 10

ATTACK

† **Morningstar**: +9 to hit d8+2hp.

† **Bronze claw**: +9 to hit d6hp.

SPECIAL

† **Stealth**: 3 in 6.

† **Sleight of hand**: 3 in 6.

Seekingbrother Oc

A CLERIC AND MENDICANT of a distant faith, with tin-bordered peridots glued to his shorn skull.

HD 6 **HP** 18 **SPEED** 120'

ARMOR 18

MORALE 7

ATTACK

† *Mace-and-chain*: +1 to hit d6hp.

† *Spells*: *Command* (x2), *Cure Light Wounds*, *Silence 15' Radius*, *Heat Metal*, *Heroism*, *Dispel Magic* (x2).

Nick Viscid

A CALLOW FIGHTER whose assets include barrels of flaming oil and a *pair of steppe borzois* named Spackwick and Trash.

HD 5 **HP** 25 **SPEED** 120'

ARMOR 17

MORALE 7

ATTACK

† *Longbow*: +6 to hit d6hp. If flaming: d4 more.

† *Bastard sword*: +6 to hit d8+1hp.

† Also carries torches and 10 *jars of oil*.

Spackwick and Trash

HD 2 **HP** 10 **SPEED** 140'

ARMOR 15

MORALE 8

ATTACK

† *Bite*: +3 to hit 2d4+1hp.

Scrother of the Wheatpig Vale

A SMILING MOUNTEBANK in particolored motley. His moustache wax and main gauche are both steeped in a love potion of inconstant efficacy.

HD 5 **HP** 20 **SPEED** 120'

ARMOR 14

MORALE 5

ATTACK

† *Dagger*: +1 to hit d4hp.

† *Crossbow*: +2 to hit d6hp.

† *Short sword/Main gauche*: +1 to hit d6hp (Successful stab on the first hit indicates a *Charm* effect—save at +5).

† *Sneak attack* x6.

SPECIAL

† *Stealth*: 4 in 6.

† *Sleight of hand*: 5 in 6.

Avalanche

Accumulated crystalline water vapor coaxed by gravity into an attempt to entomb you. An avalanche is not a creature but may be treated as one for the purposes of initiative, etc. It may help to make a little sketch and keep track of where the wavefront of the avalanche is in relation to the party.

HD 10 **HP** 50 **SPEED** 180'

ARMOR 12

MORALE n/a

ATTACK (All attacks that apply are used each round)

† *Trip/Fall*: This actually represents the possibility of stumbling or losing your footing while running away from an avalanche—*it affects all creatures running from the avalanche* and requires a save vs Breath Weapon from everyone to avoid falling. A successful Bushcraft roll will allow a character to reroll a failed save once.

† *Engulf*: This "attack" is used against any creatures in contact with the avalanche itself on the avalanche's turn. Save vs Breath Weapon—a failed save indicates 2d20hp of crushing damage, a successful save indicates d12hp.

DEFENSE

† Ordinary **weapons are useless** here—avalanches can only take damage by magic or mechanisms that would affect an epic wave of homicidal snow. *Magic Missile* can cut into the wavefront, and a spell like *Slow* could be cast on the front. Attacks that cause extreme heat (much more than a torch or lantern) or explosions can eat into the front, and spells like *Dig* and *Move Earth* are a good bet.

SPECIAL

† The avalanche will usually start (d4+1) x 100 feet from the party and automatically **lose d20hp per round** until "dead".

† These hit points only represent the part of a larger avalanche that might hurt a small party (20-60 feet of the whole front), reducing this part to zero does not affect the avalanche as a whole, which might be 2-10 times the size as the part which puts travelers in immediate danger.

† An avalanche's **height** is equal to half its current hit points—getting safely above it obviously allows victims to escape unscathed.

BELPHEGOR

BELPHEGOR IS MASTER OF BEASTS, the Disputer, he walks on the legs of a goat, his head thrice-crowned: raven, stag, great wolf. 200' tall, he is the Bringer of Terror, the Hunter of All, his throne is the mountain. The three witches, Thorn, Frost, and Dread seek to bring him to this world, and, through him, destruction beyond measure.

His great *foe is Nidhoggr*, for she is the story of his coming, and he repudiates all documentation.

HD 25 **HP*** each head: 100 torso: 155 each leg: 100 each arm: 100 **SPEED** 240'

ARMOR 20

MORALE 12

*Depleting the hit points of the torso or every head kills the creature. Depleting the hit points of any other body part nullifies that part's attacks and makes it less maneuverable, but has no effect on its overall health.

ATTACKS (5 attacks per round)

† *Bite attacks* (each may be used only once per round).

† *Wolf's bite*: +13 to hit 2d12hp.

† *Gore*: +13 to hit d20hp.

† *Raven's beak*: Impale +13 to hit 4d6hp.

† *Great caw*: save vs Breath Weapon or take d20hp sonic damage and deafened for 2 weeks. Con check in two weeks—failure indicates permanent deafness (Twice/day).

† *Crush/punch/claw*: +13 to hit 3d6hp.

† All *animals* native to the Devoured Land, save for serpents, *obey* Belphegor and will be attracted when he is summoned, and will attack his foes.

DEFENSE

† Each head *saves separately* for effects like illusions, charm, etc. that target the brain or sensory organs.

† 5 times/day, Belphegor may sacrifice a number of hit points (from any body part) equal to the level of the caster to *ignore a spell effect*—this may be announced after the spell is cast and any relevant save is made.

† Belphegor's body is so large that most weapons and spells can only target *one body part at a time*. If the hit points of the legs, arms, or a head are depleted, Nidhoggr will be unable to use that limb until it heals, but will probably fight on, since he'll be pretty pissed.

SPECIAL

† Any who look upon Belphegor and survive *gain +1 Wisdom* permanently.

Bjära

The bjära, or troll-cat, is a hare-like animal compounded by witches from a gelatinous dough of human fat, skin and fingernails and baked in a stony oven. It sucks milk from the teats of livestock and runs to a milk pail atop a high hill where other bjära gather to spit it out. When the gathered bjära have filled the bucket with enough stolen milk to drown a rabbit or a child, they seek out rabbits or children and do just that. They then drag the victims to the homes of their mother-witches to be eaten.

HD 2 **HP** 10 **SPEED** 120'
ARMOR 16
MORALE 6
ATTACK
† *Bite*: +2 to hit 2d4hp.
DEFENSE
† If slain, the bjära *explodes* in a 10' spray of cursed milk doing 2d6 damage to any creature nearby.
SPECIAL
† The bjära can *climb any surface*.
† Bjära can *imitate the voice* of any creature and will use this ability to lure its prey or enemies into avalanches or other hazards.

Boars

BOARS AREN'T TERRIBLY EXCITING, thus the name—unless you're a Maggot Sister, then they kill and eat people for you. Also a baby boar is called a "squeaker" which is pretty cute.

HD 2 **HP** 10 **SPEED** 120'

ARMOR 14

MORALE 8

ATTACK

† *Bite*: +2 to hit 2d4hp.

Crows

THE CROW IS GREEDY and will take shiny things. Coins, the eyes from your face. They find it's easier in the other order. They come quietly to sleepers, playing ordinary birds, simultaneously drive their beaks into their victim's eyes, then fly off, track them, come back later when they've met with misfortune and take all their silver. No one knows what they will buy.

Typical Crow

HD 1 **HP** 4 **SPEED** 240'
ARMOR 16 (high Dex)
MORALE 4
ATTACK
† *Eye gouge*: +1 or autohit on a helpless victim—d6hp and victim is blinded in one eye. Victim must make a Con check each morning to restore sight, failing 3 times in a row means the eye is permanently useless. Also: three successful gouges on the same target or a single natural 20 means the eye has been removed.
DEFENSE
† Crows are *allied to death*. They cannot be harmed by those who have never killed another of their same species.
SPECIAL
† *Sleight of hand* (pick pocket small items, sever cords, etc.) 3 in 6.
† *Stealth* 4 in 6.

Murder of Crows (more than 7 crows)

HD 4–10 (more crows = more HD) **HP** 16-40
SPEED 240'
ARMOR 16 (high Dex)
MORALE 5

ATTACKS (4 Attacks per round)
† *Eye gouge*: +1 or autohit on a helpless victim—d6hp and victim is blinded in one eye. Victim must make a Con check each morning to restore sight, failing 3 times in a row means the eye is permanently useless and cannot be healed short of regenerating magic. Also: three successful gouges on the same target or a single natural 20 means the eye has been removed.
DEFENSE
† Crows are *allied to death*. They cannot be harmed by those who have never killed another of their own species.
SPECIAL
† *Sleight of hand* (pick pocket small items, sever cords, etc.) 5 in 6.

Black Sky

THIS CROW SCHEMES to find great hoards, waits patiently and attacks adventurers only after they've uncovered wealth.

HD 2 **HP** 10 **SPEED** 240'
ARMOR 16 (high Dex)
MORALE 5
ATTACK
† ***Eye gouge***: +4 or autohit on a helpless victim—d6hp and victim is blinded in one eye. Victim must make a Con check each morning to restore sight, failing 3 times in a row means the eye is permanently useless and cannot be healed short of regenerating magic. Also: three successful gouges on the same target means the eye has been removed.
† ***Tongue bite***: +4 to hit d4hp and victim cannot speak. Victim must make a Con check each morning to restore speech, failing 3 times in a row means the tongue is permanently useless. Also: three successful gouges on the same target means the tongue has been removed. Black Sky knows how to pick out spell-casters.
DEFENSE
† Crows are ***allied to death***. They cannot be harmed by those who have never killed another of their same species.
SPECIAL
† ***Sleight of hand*** (pick pocket small items, sever cords, etc.) 5 in 6.
† ***Stealth*** 5 in 6.

Vorvik

THIS CROW WORKS in concert with the wolf, Skintaster, scouting out, crippling, and picking clean her pack's victims.

HD 2 **HP** 10 **SPEED** 240'
ARMOR 16 (high Dex)
MORALE 6
ATTACK
† ***Eye gouge***: +3 or autohit on a helpless victim—d6hp and victim is blinded in one eye. Victim must make a Con check each morning to restore sight, failing 3 times in a row means the eye is permanently useless and cannot be healed short of regenerating magic. Also: three successful gouges on the same target means the eye has been removed.
DEFENSE
† Crows are ***allied to death***. They cannot be harmed by those who have never killed another of their same species.
SPECIAL
† ***Sleight of hand*** (pick pocket small items, sever cords, etc.) 5 in 6.
† ***Stealth*** 5 in 6.

Ear Eater

IS FAMILIAR TO THE WITCH, Dread, and is listed alongside her.

Dogs

I presume the reader is familiar with the goals and character of dogs. They are among the few animals who were no different in days past, nor in the Devoured Land, which maintains the orders and agreements of that time. Dogs are and have always been the way they are—which is probably why we keep them around. They do not like wolves, and wolves do not like them.

HD 2 **HP** 10 **Speed** 130'

Armor 15

Morale 10

Attack

† **Bite**: +3 to hit 2d4+1hp.

Defense

† Amazon dogs are occasionally fitted with a kind of **studded leather** harness which

Drowning Demons

IT IS SAID COLD RIVERS LEAD to the homes of the damned, and it is well-known that the damned are lonely. Drowning demons come from the water, slithering and bounding, seeking souls, they take the living and drag them down. They attack with guilt and shame but are more ashamed of themselves—they evaporate when their true name is spoken, they cannot abide being known.

HD 7 **HP** 35 **SPEED** 180'

ARMOR 16 (Though it won't come up much)

MORALE 11

ATTACK

† **Grapple**: +7 to hit with 16 Str. Successfully grappled characters will be dragged to the nearest body of water and drowned. If you don't have a mechanic for drowning, you can make it a save vs Poison or take d8 damage each round.

DEFENSE

† Drowning demons can usually **only be hurt by attacks which would turn water to steam or ice**, or otherwise disrupt the flow of water. Sufficiently heated metal weapons will do damage as normal. *Purify Food and Drink* will kill one.

† Drowning demons **evaporate when their true name is spoken**—there are 20 drowning demons, so if a player learns the name of one, you can use that fact to calculate the odds that the name they speak is the right one. Like if you know the name of three, you have a 3 in 20 chance that's the one you're fighting.

FROST GIANTS
of the Hatemountain

Colossal beyond all experience, towering two hundred feet, skin cracked, mouths slavering black, eyes bleeding black. Their manes are taken by winds unknown at our layer of the troposphere, their every step is thunder, their fists white elephants, their hearts cold engines. They are terrible news, like the resentful echoes of abandoned faiths. Like you would be, if a swarm of talking lice had taken your parents' planet from them and you had to live in a mountain made of hate. They have immense treasure hoards and feed on reindeer and whales.

action if she wants to improve her position, not just to hang on in the same position.

† In addition, each giant has **one of the following traits**, always active (roll d10):

1. *Circle of Dead Children*: Humans and demihumans under thirteen winters die in a 50' radius.
2. *Extreme Noise Terror*: Releases a bellow which deafens those around unless they save vs Paralysis.
3. *Gore Beyond Necropsy*: Any piercing wound to the giant shoots a fountain of blood, save vs Breath Weapon or take d10 drowning damage.
4. *Kaaos*: Flora and fauna mutate for 100 feet around them as if misshaped (see: **Misshaped Animals**, pg 47).
5. *Locusts*: swarm precedes them.
6. *Mortification*: Those who look upon them must save vs Magic or stab themselves.

IF YOU HAVE A copy of *Broodmother Sky Fortress*, these giants may be treated as those in terms of stats, otherwise:

HD 20 **HP*** Each arm 70

Each leg 100 Torso 90 Head 60 **SPEED** 240'

ARMOR 20

MORALE 11

*Depleting the hp of the torso or head kills the creature. Depleting the hp of any other body part nullifies that part's attacks and makes it less maneuverable, but has no effect on its overall health.

ATTACKS (3 attacks per round)

† **Grab**: +13 to hit d8 crushing damage.
† **Stomp or pound**: +13 to hit 5d6hp.
† **Throw a grabbed victim** (or someone climbing on the giant): 10d6hp, save vs Breath Weapon for half.
† **Eat a grabbed victim**: 4d6hp, save vs Breath Weapon to dodge the teeth and end up inside the giant's mouth.

DEFENSE

† The giants' bodies are so large that most weapons and spells can only target **one body part at a time**. If the hit points of the legs or arms are depleted, the giant will be unable to use that limb, but will probably fight on, since it'll be pretty pissed.

7. *Nausea*: Those who look upon them must save vs Poison or vomit.
8. *Phobia*: Causes Fear as spell in 50' radius.
9. *Unholy Grave*: Will rise as undead if proper rites are not performed.
10. *Zero Content*: Any writing not dedicated to the dark gods within 100' begins to burn.

SPECIAL

† For each round spent successfully **climbing on a giant** (and not attacking) a character will gain +2 to hit and damage on her strikes from the new position achieved. If the giant tries to throw someone off, saving or Dex checking against that happens on the giant's turn, not the PCs, so the character only needs to use an

Goat

THE GOAT ENJOYS ITS TIME on the mortal plane. If it is stubborn it is only because it is hungry for life. Goats despise trolls and in turn trolls despise goats more. While it is not true that goats may eat anything, they have been known to ruminate on a wide variety of topics. Those casting *Speak with Animals* and consulting a goat on any topic will likely be confronted with a well-developed (if not always well-conceived) treatment of the subject.

HD 1-3 **HP** 5-15 **SPEED** 120'

ARMOR 14

MORALE 11

ATTACK

† *Gore* +2 to hit 2d6hp.

† *Charging gore* (only at the start of combat) +6 to hit 4d6hp.

DEFENSE

† *Goats* that have slain a troll regenerate at 4hp per round.

SPECIAL

† *Trolls* cannot heal wounds inflicted by goat horns.

Horses

LIKE DOGS, HORSES ARE NOBLE, constant creatures, at least insofar as humans measure such things. There were once more wild horses here—the Amazons offered to enslave them, the wolves offered to eat them. They made the only choice they could. The most common breed in the Devoured Land is the fjord horse—strong, thick necked, sure-footed on slopes—for convenience' sake, I put their stats here.

HD 3 **HP** 9 **SPEED** 240'

ARMOR 15

MORALE 8

ATTACKS (3 attacks per round)

† **Hoof**: +3 to hit d6hp (only two hoofs per round).

† **Bite**: +3 to hit d4hp.

King Ovv

OVV WAS THE RULER OF THE FORGOTTEN civilization that built the Dim Fortress in aeons so remote even the sister-witches recall it only as you remember the texture of the first carpet you crawled. His kingdom was awful, and he was a despot—the kind of man who inspired gods to invent death by old age. But he got in under the wire. All his subjects and enemies long dead, his stronghold entombed, he sits still atop the Darkthrone, ten feet tall, clutching his sword, waiting for someone to be a bastard to.

HD 20 **HP** 150 **SPEED** 120'

ARMOR 18

MORALE 12

ATTACKS (4 attacks per round)

† *Great sword*: +13 to hit d10+4hp. This unholy sword—*Mutilator*—is forged from pure ektesvarsk.

† *Choke*: +13 to hit d6+3hp plus grapple with 18 Str.

DEFENSE

† Mutilator is **immune to magic** and extends this protection to King Ovv so long as he holds it.

† If King Ovv is reduced to zero hit points he will **keep fighting** so long as he still clutches Mutilator. Only when separated from the blade will he finally rest.

SPECIAL

† *Mutilator* grants the abilities listed above (including +1 to damage) to anyone using it. However, after the first day of use, the wielder will wake up with King Ovv's hand (which will try to kill them). The owner of the blade will turn into Ovv at the rate of 6 inches per day, after the hand, then the arm, then the shoulder, then one half of the neck, then half of the head, then the other half (at which point the character becomes an NPC). Getting rid of the blade stops the spread of Ovv but doesn't reverse the transformation—*Remove Curse* or the like can remove 6 inches of infection per casting.

Misshaped Animals

HD 1-8 **HP** 5-40 **SPEED** roll d6:
(1–2: 60', 3–5: 120', 6: 180')
ARMOR 8+d10
MORALE 7
ATTACK
† **Claw**, **bite** or **gore** usually at a to hit bonus
   equal to the creature's HD. Roll d4 when
   creating the misshaped animal to see how
   much damage the animal's attack does:
   1. d4hp
   2. d6hp
   3. d8hp
   4. d10hp

d100 Misshaped Animals

1–3	Bat	53–54	Lynx
4–5	Beetle	55–56	Mantis
6–8	Boar	57–58	Mole
9–10	Butterfly	59–60	Mouse
11–12	Cat	61–63	Newt
13–14	Centipede	64–65	Otter
15–16	Cock	66–67	Owl
17–19	Crow	68–69	Pheasant
20–21	Dog	70–71	Pig
22–23	Dove	72–74	Polar bear
24–25	Donkey	75–76	Rat
26–28	Eagle	77–79	Scorpion
29–31	Ferret	80–81	Serpent
32–33	Fly	82–83	Sheep
34–35	Fox	84–85	Slug
36–38	Frog/Toad	86–87	Spider
39–40	Goat	88	Snow leopard
41–43	Hare/rabbit	89–91	Stag
44–46	Heron	92–94	Swan
47–48	Horse	95–96	Turtle
49–50	Insect (any)	97–98	Whale
51–52	Jellyfish	99–00	Wolf

WHEN ANYTHING IMMORTAL IS SLAIN, their essence bastardizes the nearby waters and those that taste them are made new and monstrous. The thousand casualties of hundreds of unimagined wars enrich the Devoured Land and feed the Misshaping Pools (see Deformations of the Misshaping Pool, pg 133).

Flying animals can almost never fly again after being misshaped, small creatures tend to bloat to at least the size of dogs, both land-dwelling and aquatic creatures may become amphibious. The kind of animal is up to you, or you can roll.

the Necrobutcher

BRINGER OF HATE, INITIATOR, embroiling you tenthousandfold in the ceremonies of grief. One of the three Cryptic Trinity, unliving servants of King Ovv, who are indescribable. 35' tall. Just show the players the artwork and roll initiative.

HD 15 **HP*** head: 25 torso: 100
each leg: 25 each arm: 20
SPEED 120'
ARMOR 15
MORALE 12

*Depleting the hp of the torso or head kills the creature. Depleting the hp of any other body part nullifies that part's attacks and makes it less maneuverable, but has no effect on its overall health.

ATTACKS (2 attacks per round)

† *Fork poke*: +8 to hit d10hp and (human sized or smaller) victim is *shoved* in the mound of organs in the Necrobutcher's chest cavity. Str check each round to escape or take d6 crushing damage.

† *Knife*: +8 to hit 3d6hp.

† *Stomp*: +8 to hit, 2d6 damage if necessary.

† *Grapple and swallow*: +8 to hit, otherwise as Fork Poke except digestive acid damage instead of crushing damage.

SPECIAL

† Within the mound of blasphemous organs inside the Necrobutcher's torso cavity there is a *bile sac* which, if punctured (15hp) will begin to leak acidic bile doing 2d6hp per round to whatever it touches. A Search roll is required to locate it if a player has the idea to look for it and sufficient anatomical knowledge.

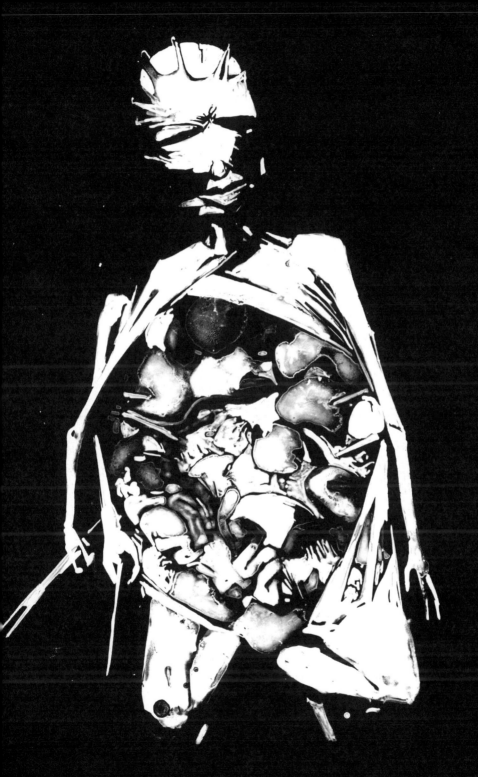

#

NIDHOGGR, CALLED THE GLISTENING ONE and called Malice Striker, is the wyrm who gnaws at a cage woven from the boneroots of the earth and sucks the blood of corpses. 250' long, five headed, grown from the severed hand of a vanished god, her only living acquaintance is the marmot, *Ratatoskr*, who comes down into the Dim Fortress, and pro- vokes her with gossip. She despises our world, and does not know our world. Her heads are called The Twisting One, The One Who Wears A Mask, The Seeker Below, Greybeneath, The One Who Gives You A Gift And That Gift Is Sleep.

Her *foe is Belphegor*, the Beast, despised since the day before all days; those who can read the skins of serpents know that her skin speaks the story of the end of all that now is.

HD 25 **HP*** EACH head: 100 torso: 200 each leg: 100 tail: 100 **SPEED** 120'

ARMOR 20

MORALE 12

ATTACKS (5 attacks per round)

† **Bite**: +13 to hit 2d12hp.

† **Tail sweep**: (only targets behind) +10 to hit d2ohp.

† **Swallow**: +13 to grapple, then d12 damage per round from stomach acid.

† **Breath weapons**—save vs Breath Weapon in all cases, each can be used twice per day:

1. *The Twisting One*: (Chill wind) d100hp from frost.

2. *The One Who Wears A Mask*: (Radiation) Grow 4 arms that try to choke you each round—4 attacks at +10 to hit d12hp.

3. *The Seeker Below*: (Projectile Vomit) d100hp fragments of bone shrapnel and stomach acid.

4. *Greybeneath*: (Shriek) d2ohp sonic damage and deafened for 2 weeks. Con check in two weeks—failure indicates permanent deafness.

5. *The One Who Gives You A Gift And That Gift Is Sleep*: (Soporific cloud) Fall asleep for d4 turns. Damage equal to half of existing hp will awake the sleeper.

*Depleting the hp of the torso or every head kills the creature. Depleting the hp of any other body part nullifies that part's attacks and makes it less maneuverable, but has no effect on its overall health.

DEFENSE

† **Each head saves separately** for effects like illusions, charm, etc. that target the brain or sensory organs.

† 3 times/day, Nidhoggr may **sacrifice** a number of hit points (from any body part) equal to the level of the caster to **ignore a spell effect**—this may be announced after the spell is cast and any relevant save is made.

† Nidhoggr's body is so large that most weapons and spells can only **target one body part at a time**. If the hit points of the legs or a head are depleted, Nidhoggr will be unable to use that limb until it heals, but will probably fight on, since she'll be pretty pissed.

SPECIAL

† Any who look upon Nidhoggr and survive **gain +1 Wisdom** permanently.

† Nidhoggr's **skin** (see Serpents, pg 62), if studied, offers clues to the story of how the world will end—practically speaking, this means it describes where many pivotal objects, creatures and people that might trigger the last war are hidden.

the Noctambulant

MOTHERTWISTER, ANNIHILATOR, the eons inseminated with agony untold. Second of the Cryptic Trinity, unspeakable. Looks like that picture. 17' tall, 40' long. Attacks on sight.

HD 13 **HP*** head: 15 torso: 30
each leg: 20 each arm: 20 **SPEED** 140'
ARMOR 17
MORALE 12
*Depleting the hp of the torso or head kills the creature. Depleting the hp of any other body part nullifies that part's attacks and makes it less maneuverable, but has no effect on its overall health.

ATTACKS (2 attacks per round)

† **Grapple**: +7 to hit d4hp. 18 Str.

† **Remove bones**: once a foe is grappled, the Noctambulant may reach with its strange fingers down its throat and remove its bones. First round it will remove the bones from one arm, second the other, then each leg, then finally the spine (which causes death).

SPECIAL

† Moves **100% silently**.

† Can **climb** any wall.

† Can **squeeze through** any opening at least 3' wide.

53

 Owls

THE HOLY MEN who have encountered owls in the bleak forests surrounding the mountains claim they are avatars of Belphegor, Lord of Hate and Beasts.

The truth is that **owls are the opposite of serpents**—while the crawling reptiles form a record of the continuous conversation reality has about itself to itself, owls are **eaters of knowledge and bringers of ignorance**. In our world, they manifest as a parasitic, semi-sentient extradimensional infection that lives inside the eyes of what were once ordinary day-hunting apex raptors (falcons, ospreys, eagles, harriers, hawks, etc.) deforming their faces and eating their souls.

Their scheme unfolds by the following means:

THE FIRST OWL a party encounters will be, in itself, harmless (unless they are encountering Tormentor with the witch named Frost, see below). It may be, as in *The Monolith from Beyond Space and Time*, an unsettling effigy of an owl or owls. It may be, as in any casual description of a forest, a passing detail given by the game master; it may be an owl in a dream (in the dream it will be eating a snake). If the first owl appears in physical form it will be nothing but an owl—with the game statistics of a common bird of prey.

THE SECOND OWL will appear soon after the first time any observer of the first owl thinks the word "owl". In game terms, this means shortly after the *player* (not the PC) uses the word "owl" during the game—in dialogue, when describing an action, or any other time in-game (whether "Look I made an owl out of Funions" and other during-game table chatter counts, and where the line between play and chatter is, is entirely up to Referee. If this is likely to cause discord with your group, do not play LotFP). If a random encounter or location description indicates an owl and no-one's said the word, this will simply indicate the sound of an owl hooting "You hear 'Who?' Who?' in the forest..."—which may prompt someone to say "owl" and thus summon it.

This second owl will not appear in any obviously supernatural fashion—it will emerge from a behind the shadow of a rafter, be found waiting on the edge of a bed in a room the PCs have just entered, etc. **It will wait a suitably creepy amount of time and then attack.**

Although the physical effect of this encounter is likely to be negligible, the **secret purpose of the animal is to steal a word** (and thus a system of ideas) from the victim on behalf of its parliament before it dies. This theft is unavoidable and happens as soon as any confrontation with the owl (initiative roll, backstab, spell cast at the owl, etc.) begins.

The stolen word will fit the following parameters:

1. It will be a word the player has **recently used**.
2. It will be a word whose presence **will be missed**, either in the current situation ("idol", "goblin", "fortress") or forever ("door", "mother", "trap", "mile").
3. It can only be a magical word (a command word or an element of one of the Power Word spells, for example) if a spellcaster rolls a natural 1 on a d20 or d100 during the encounter.
4. It will **not be any word the owls already possess**. Owls of the Devoured Land already know: "barn", "ghost", "church", "death", "hiss", "hobgoblin", "gold", "silver", "white", "night", "rat", "screech", "straw", "monkey", "delicate", "owl" and, of course, "who".

The word is gone from the victim's mind. The character may not say the word or even think it. The concept occupies a void at the intersection of related ideas in the character's mental map. Circumlocutions such as "the small greenish thing that's like a gnome only uglier and trying to hit me" are acceptable.

AFTER THE ENCOUNTER with the second owl, **THE THIRD AND ALL SUBSEQUENT OWLS** appear (as above) in response to the player saying "owl". The total number of pursuing owls will precisely match the total number of times the player uses the

After a few thousand more victims, the owls may be able to communicate in something resembling language. This will in no way make them less hostile or desperate to return to their home. The only way to get the words back is to kill every owl in the parliament.

Different parliaments possess different sets of words, though as they can only steal words from humanoids, they do not esteem one another and occasionally compete. Owls outside the Devoured Land have forgotten their true nature, and behave like ordinary birds. Usually.

Typical Owl

HD 1 **HP** 4 **SPEED** 240'
ARMOR 14 (high Dex)
MORALE 7
ATTACK
† *Claw*: +2 to hit d4hp.
† Automatically *steals a word* (see above) when encounter begins.

word "owl" after and during the encounter with the second owl. Whether the owls appear one by one or in groups can be determined by the Referee. (The Alfred Hitchcock film "The Birds" is a good example of a non-silly execution of this idea.) Each owl will behave as the second owl did, attacking and stealing a new word.

Owls will continue to be summoned by the word "owl" for the rest of the victim's life. No-one will ever encounter an owl otherwise—any alleged "owl" appearing outside the scheme described here is probably a doppelganger, minor demon or otherwise not what it seems—with the exception of witches' familiars.

The owls' ultimate goal is to collect enough native concepts to understand the dimension they inhabit and return to their own. They can only speak or understand words they have stolen.

Stryx

STRYX LEADS THE OLDEST and largest parliament in the Devoured Land. Its vocabulary is large. The Parliament has 42 members at present.

HD 3 **HP** 12 **SPEED** 240'
ARMOR 15 (high Dex)
MORALE 8
ATTACK
† *Claw*: +5 to hit d6hp.
† Automatically *steals a word* (see above) when encounter begins.

Tormentor

TORMENTOR IS FAMILIAR to the witch, Frost, and is listed alongside her.

Pearlholders

THE PEARLHOLDERS ARE A STOLID AND ANCIENT CULT, and hold to a strict and Kantian code: they forbid any action that would bring ill were it to be copied by all men, women, and children. The provocatively meager sartorial style of the Amazons is a particular source of consternation in the Devoured Lands and each Pearlholder goes about with heavy cloaks (nudity being inappropriate for the young and frail), to forcibly swaddle and enswathe them, lest young people be driven to distraction. They are named for the carved and runic **trollpearls** they carry, which prevent all symmetries—making them immune to any weapon or moral law they attack another with.

The Pearlholders are among the few who willingly abandon cities and farms to traverse the Devoured Land, seeking to bring transgressors low and build tall churches upon their graves. To this end they **fondle and feed trolls**, whose talent for disruption they seek to funnel toward the annihilation of the unsanctioned.

In addition to the usual paraphernalia of willing subjugation, **each Pearlholder church** possesses two unique architectural features:

† A **Giftschrank** (or "poison cabinet")—a collection of forbidden texts (some theological, scientific or practical, but mostly fiction and poetry) to which have been added Pearlholder marginalia in the form of counter-texts which decry, undermine and contest all that is inscribed therein.

† An octagonal **Baptisterium** containing a vast font suitable for the submersion and anointment of trolls in a milky liquid composed of the seed and vital fluids of Pearlholders known as "chrism".

Typical Pearlholder

HD 2 **HP** 8 **SPEED** 120'
ARMOR 12
MORALE 6
ATTACK

† Various **weapons** at +2 to hit d6hp. Especially blunt ones.

DEFENSE

† Trollpearls make the Pearlholders **immune** to any specific weapon, kind of attack or spell they have already employed against the target. So once a Pearlholder attacks you with a garrote, they are immune to garrote attacks from you, once a Pearlholder attacks you with *Hold Person*, you cannot successfully attack them with *Hold Person*.

SPECIAL

† The Trollpearls **only work for initiates** of their Church.

† Some Pearlholders are **Clerics** or **Thieves**, they will usually be 2nd level.

† Pearlholders never go out at night.

the Plaguewielder

THIRD OF THE CRYPTIC TRINITY. Emptier, inviter of contagion, dissolver. Language is insufficient to express this inexorable brutality, so I drew a picture. 30' tall.

HD 16 **HP*** head: 30 torso: 100
each leg: 30 each arm: 30 **SPEED** 110'
ARMOR 17
MORALE 12

*Depleting the hp of the torso or head kills the creature. Depleting the hp of any other body part nullifies that part's attacks and makes it less maneuverable, but has no effect on its overall health.

ATTACKS (2 attacks per round)

† *Plague touch*: +7 to hit save vs Poison or contract Seething Pustules (see below).

DEFENSE

† *Magic that affects disease* will cause hit point damage to the Plaguewielder equal to d8+the spell's level.

† *Immune to disease*.

Seething Pustules

SICKENING BOILS erupt from the victim's skin and *explode* for d10 damage to everyone within 15' (once every d6 hours). Anyone within the blast must save or contract the illness. Can only be cured by magic.

Ratatostr

Scholars have proposed theories about the implications of this slanderous marmot, but none have been confirmed. Only this is certain—he is a gossiper and messenger and a tumbler, and brings scurrilous **reports down to Nidhoggr**, the Wyrm from all over the Devoured Land, enraging her against all things. He has done so since the first day of the Wyrm's imprisonment.

HD 2 **HP** 10 **SPEED** 240'

ARMOR 16 (high Dex)

MORALE 5

ATTACK

† *Mass Suggestion* at will.

† *Howl of the Moon* at will—if this spell needs to be delivered forcibly, Ratatoskr makes **touch attacks** at +4. Unlike an ordinary *Howl* spell, this spell need not be used at night.

DEFENSE

† Ratatoskr is older than all the gods, so is **immune to divine magic**.

SPECIAL

† Ratatoskr **knows everything** there is to know about everyone, but doesn't really care or do much about it.

† If it can be climbed, Ratatoskr **can climb** it.

Rats

Rats are envious, they squirm and need. They love for humans to build homes, so that they can take them over—thus do they encourage both civilization and its dissolution. They eat clothes, supplies, armor straps—whatever allows a party to survive outside the close society of others. They detest the Frostbitten Moons, for these Amazons collect rats in vast quantities to feed their warmistress' snakes.

Rat Swarm

HD 5-10 **HP** 20-40 **Speed** 180'
Armor 12 **Morale** 11
Attacks (3 attacks per round)
† **Bite**: +5-10 to hit (as HD) d4hp plus save vs Poison or contract Nest Fever (see below).
Special
† If the swarm has a **leader rat**, it gains one extra attack per HD of the leader.

Ribboned Jenny

A champion rat of the Rottingkroner fighting pits. She has bad memories of the hands of humans and will see them brought low.
HD 2 **HP** 4 **Speed** 180'
Armor 12 **Morale** 11
Attack
† **Bite**: +2 to hit d6hp and save vs Poison or contract Nest Fever (see below).
Special
† If Ribboned Jenny **joins a swarm** and forgoes her own action, the swarm gains two extra attacks per round for a total of 5.

Nest Fever

The most common illness carried by rats of the Devoured Land—it has an incubation period of 24 hours (i.e. take damage after 24 hours), an interval of 24 hours (i.e. save again every 24 hours or take damage) and a duration equal to (20 minus the victim's Con) days (i.e. the infection ends after that many days). Each failed save causes **d4 hit points** of damage.

Blasphemer

Despises churches. His swarm will seek holy symbols, befoul holy water, tear holy books apart.
HD 1 **HP** 2 **Speed** 180'
Armor 12 **Morale** 11
Attack
† **Bite**: +2 to hit d6hp and save vs Poison or contract Nest Fever (see below).
Special
† If Blasphemer **joins a swarm** and forgoes his own action, the swarm gains an extra attack per round for a total of 4.
† Blasphemer may **utter** an *Unholy Word* (as the spell) once per week. So be careful out there.
† Blasphemer is effectively **covered in unholy water** at all times.

Serpents

THE WORLD ENGAGES in a continuous monologue about itself to itself and the tongue of this discourse is the serpent. All *serpents are knowledge incarnate*—the more exotic the snake, the more esoteric the facts revealed when their skins are read by those who know the language of scales (known to all witches, and many who have studied under them). As such, they seek only incident—the raw material from which the records and fictions that form their bodies are produced. That is why snakes only appear at interesting moments. The empress of all serpents is *Nidhoggr*, who is the story of the end of the world.

Black Tongue

PREFERS TO STRIKE HORSES in full gallop, or the hands of climbers. His followers each attack a different limb of a different party member—this tends to improve stories immensely—then retreat as fast as possible.

HD 2 **HP** 8 **SPEED** 90'
ARMOR 14 **MORALE** 9
ATTACK

† **Bite**: +4 to hit d8hp and save vs Poison each round until a save is made, taking 4hp per failed save. If any saves are failed the affected body part will swell grotesquely and the character will take 10hp every morning until it is treated.

DEFENSE

† Black Tongue's glittering skin *reflects all magic* back on the caster.

SPECIAL

† If read, Black Tongue is a *guide to medicinal herbs* in the Devoured Land.

Typical Serpent

HD 1 **HP** 5 **SPEED** 90'
ARMOR 14 **MORALE** 8
ATTACK

† **Bite**: +2 to hit d4hp and save vs Poison each round until a save is made, taking 2hp per failed save. If any saves are failed the affected body part will swell grotesquely and the character will take 5hp every morning until it is treated.

SPECIAL

† If read, typical **serpent skins** will reveal, like, the tale of a duchess whose lover goes East, or a gardening book.

Sermon

LEADS THE SERPENTS that infest the bed and belongings of Jex Amon, warmistress of the Frostbitten Moons and is listed alongside her.

Snakkur

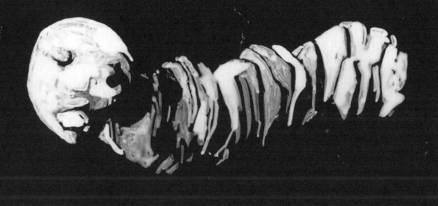

LIKE THE BJÄRA, THE SNAKKUR is a milk-stealing golem built by witches. It is made from a rib wrapped in stolen wool, brought to life with the tears of unwed mothers and fouled communion wine, and resembles a worm as wide as a wrist with a twisted child-like face.

In addition to milk, the snakkur crawls into the mouths of men by night and sucks up their undigested food, regurgitating it into the mouths of their mother-witches, whose teeth are too aged to properly chew.

HD 2 **HP** 10 **SPEED** 120'
ARMOR 14
MORALE 8
ATTACK
† *Choke*: +2 to hit, crawl into mouth doing d4 choking damage per round until removed. The damage is doubled if the target is asleep or unconscious when the snakkur enters them.
SPECIAL
† The snakkur can *climb* any surface.

Snow Leopards

AT SOME POINT in the last century, a breeding pair of these cats imported from the East and intended for a foppish zoo escaped on the road from Rottingkroner. They have adapted well. The males have crystalline teeth. Females now prize the taste of the hands of Amazons. Honestly, they have no time for all these other animals and their bullshit and just want to be left alone and/or eat them.

Typical Snow Leopard

HD 4 **HP** 20 **SPEED** 120'

ARMOR 15

MORALE 10

ATTACKS (3 attacks per round)

† *Claw*: +4 to hit d4hp

† *Bite*: +4 to hit d8hp (Only one bite per round)

† If two claw attacks land on the same target in the same round, the leopard may make *two more claw attacks* on its turn.

DEFENSE

† Snow Leopards *cannot be charmed or deceived* by Western magic.

SPECIAL

† *Stealth*: 4 in 6.

Transcending Massacre

WANTS HER TERRITORY free of any lifeform larger than a rabbit. She might negotiate toward this end if there's anything left to negotiate with after her drift's initial (terrifying, strategic) pounce. She has noticed that humans tend to flee when their fingers are removed, and so has learned to target them.

HD 6 **HP** 30 **SPEED** 120'

ARMOR 15

MORALE 11

ATTACKS (3 attacks per round)

† *Claw*: +6 to hit d6hp

† *Bite*: +6 to hit d10hp (Only one bite per round)

† If two claw attacks land on the same target in the same round, the leopard may make *two more claw attacks* on its turn.

† *Finger-bite*: +6 to hit d4hp, target loses one finger per hp of damage—counts as two attacks. These do not come back with ordinary *Cure Wounds* spells—they require regeneration or the like. (Only one bite per round)

DEFENSE

† Snow Leopards *cannot be charmed or deceived* by Western magic.

SPECIAL

† *Stealth*: 3 in 6.

Unfolding-And-Immanent-Mercy

PERPHAPS IN RESPONSE to the echo of an ancestral imperative, the leopards that attend Unfolding-And-Immanent-Mercy strike primarily at merchant caravans.

HD 5 **HP** 24 **SPEED** 120'

ARMOR 15

MORALE 10

ATTACKS (3 attacks per round)

† *Claw*: +5 to hit d4hp

† *Bite*: +5 to hit d8hp (Only one bite per round)

† If two claw attacks land on the same target in the same round, the leopard may make *two more claw attacks* on its turn.

DEFENSE

† Snow Leopards *cannot be charmed or deceived* by Western magic.

SPECIAL

† *Stealth*: 4 in 6.

All-Shall-Fall

THE CATS OF ALL-SHALL-FALL'S drift come quietly, never revealing their number, widely dispersed. They seek to subtly terrorize and disorient—a leopard may attack once, then flee, or the drift may shadow the party for an hour, at the edge of the lines of sight in every direction; anything to unnerve intruders.

HD 5 **HP** 24 **SPEED** 120'

ARMOR 15

MORALE 11

ATTACKS (3 attacks per round)

† *Claw*: +5 to hit d4hp

† *Bite*: +5 to hit d8hp (Only one bite per round)

† If two claw attacks land on the same target in the same round, the leopard may make *two more claw attacks* on its turn.

DEFENSE

† Snow Leopards *cannot be charmed or deceived* by Western magic.

SPECIAL

† *Stealth*: 5 in 6.

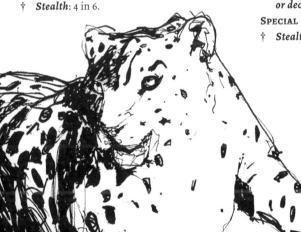

TRolLS

THERE IS NOTHING WORSE than a troll. Even in the rare case when their victims are deserving, they accomplish nothing that couldn't have been done some other way. These failed offspring of the fey and the giants stagger, 15'-20' tall, flailing with mismatched limbs across plains, desperate for release from the intricacies of existence, moaning at an apathetic sky, desiring only to stymie all endeavors, to masticate and swallow anything that does not reflect themselves.

They are worshipped by Pearlholders, who—as the oxpecker bird services the deep folds of the hippopotamus—ecstatically caress the secret places of the trolls' chapped flesh, rubbing their crust-sheathed appendages with their faces and the white chrism in the fonts of their baptisteria.

Trolls hate all goats—begrudging them their constancy and omnivorousness. Anything a troll eats turns to gold in its belly. Each is different.

Basic Troll

HD 8 **HP** 40 **SPEED** 120'

ARMOR 17

MORALE 10

ATTACKS (2 attacks per round)

† **Trollhammer**: +6 to hit d8hp or knock enemy prone.

DEFENSE

† **Regenerates** 4hp/rnd so long as anyone can see or hear it.

SPECIAL

† Belly contains d10x400sp worth of things turned to gold.

Unique Attacks

EACH TROLL'S **attacks are unique**. Make one up or simply choose a spell they can cast at-will, likely ones include (d20):

1. *Putrefy Food and Drink*
2. *Silence 15' Radius*
3. *Cause Disease*
4. *Antipathy/Sympathy*
5. *Anti-Magic Shell*
6. *Audible Glamour*
7. *Confusion*
8. *Feeblemind*
9. *Lose the Path*
10. *Forget*
11. *Slow*
12. *Holy Word*
13. *Darkness*
14. *Protection from Good*
15. *Bestow Curse*
16. *Symbol of Despair*
17. *Symbol of Insanity*
18. *False Seeing*
19. *Wall of Fog*
20. *Mirror Image*

fibbing Troll

DROPS PREY INTO A NET and is forbidden to say
true things, for his desire is to boggle and perplex.
He lives with Gruntling on Lachrymose Peak, with
a turgid, joyless face on his belly and a false and
smiling one on his shoulders.

HD 10 **HP** 50 **SPEED** 120'

ARMOR 17 **MORALE** 9

ATTACKS (2 attacks per round)

† **Suggestion** at will. If intruders appear
  on the Fibbing Troll's lair, he will try to
  get them into the Effigy Net below.

† **Trollhammer**: +6 to hit d8hp
  or knock enemy prone.

DEFENSE

† **Regenerates** 4hp/rnd so long as
  anyone can see or hear him.

SPECIAL

† **The Effigy Net** is a 10' wide 40' long 40' deep
  net stretched beneath the ice bridge where the
  Fibbing Troll dwells. It is filled 40' deep with
  small straw dolls of all its previous victims.
  Anyone falling into the net must make a
  successful Str check each round or fall 10' inside.
  After one round beneath the surface of the dolls,
  the victim must make a successful Con check
  each round or take d6 suffocation damage.

† Belly contains d10x500sp worth
  of things turned to gold.

Gruntling

CREEPS ALONG THE GROUND, sucking constantly, then, when a likely victim has been traced, hurls all over them. Anyone remarking that they have been vomited on will be set upon by the Fibbing Troll, who cannot abide any fact. She longs to cook you in a stew.

HD 10 **HP** 50 **SPEED** 120'

ARMOR 17 **MORALE** 8

ATTACKS (2 attacks per round)

† *Hurling*: Toxic vomit in 20' radius. All must save vs Breath Weapon or become increasingly disgusted and bored with life, suffering -1 to all rolls in the first round, -2 in the second, -3 in the third etc. until *Cure Disease* is cast or Gruntling is defeated.

† *Trollhammer*: +6 to hit d8hp or knock enemy prone.

DEFENSE

† *Regenerates* 4hp/rnd so long as anyone can see or hear her.

SPECIAL

† *Tracing*: Whenever, wherever this troll is mentioned, she knows who said it and where.

† Belly contains d10x500sp worth of things turned to gold.

Gutterleech

A SELF-PITYING troll covered in crawling babies.

HD 8 **HP** 40 **SPEED** 120'

ARMOR 17 **MORALE** 8

ATTACKS (2 attacks per round)

† *Entangle*: swings child by its own entrails +10 to hit, on a hit the victim is entangled.

† *Throw children*: +10 to hit d8hp

DEFENSE

† *Regenerates* 4hp/rnd so long as anyone can see or hear it.

SPECIAL

† Belly contains d10x400sp worth of things turned to gold.

Shiverer

A THIN AND TWISTING troll who eats frozen horses. He wears magic gauntlets of ektesvarsk.

HD 7 **HP** 35 **SPEED** 120'

ARMOR 17 **MORALE** 10

ATTACKS (2 attacks per round)

† *Ektesvarsk punch* +10 to hit 2d6hp

† *Disintegrates* clothes and Armor with a touch.

DEFENSE

† *Regenerates* 4hp/rnd so long as anyone can see or hear it.

SPECIAL

† Belly contains d10x400sp worth of things turned to gold.

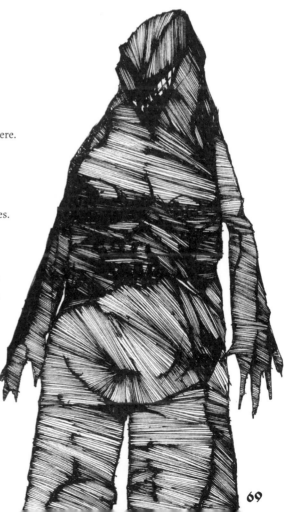

Merewolves

SOME WOMEN ARE WILD beyond comprehension. Some women will kill without weapons and drink blood from the tracks of the things they've slain— they become werewolves. Hateful, they course through the black forests, ravenous, murdering without discrimination. By day they prefer subterfuge and their original form—know them then by the fanged mouth where once was the pink center of each breast and by their yellow eyes. The Ulvenbrigad see them as sacred, they see the Ulvenbrigad as food. They are sufferers, ungovernable, they hunt alone.

HD 14 **HP** 70 **SPEED** 120' as human, 180' as wolf

ARMOR 16

MORALE 11

ATTACKS (2 attacks per round)

† (as human) **Claw** +4 to hit d6hp

† (as wolf) **Bite**: +10 to hit for 3d6hp and save vs Poison or contract lycanthropy (see below).

DEFENSE

† Werewolves can **only take damage from** silver weapons, holy water, holy magic items or clerical magic cast by a Cleric that has already successfully hurt the werewolf in some other way (they will feel their faith becoming stronger). Werewolves are **immune to arcane** magic.

SPECIAL

† Werewolves may **change from woman to wolf** at will.

Lycanthropy

IF A CHARACTER contracts lycanthropy, *Remove Curse, Cure Disease* or the like will fix it—if the condition goes untreated the character will turn into a voracious NPC wolf on the night of the next full moon (with the defenses above), and will be human in the morning. This will continue each month until the wolf draws the blood of a friend or an innocent, at which point the character will become a full werewolf, with the attacks and defense listed above (if the PC has a better attack bonus, substitute that).

Once this occurs, the **character is controlled by their appetites**—if in an inhabited area, they must kill and eat a human each day, if isolated, they must kill at least 100lbs worth of living flesh of some kind. Failure to do so within a 24-hour period means the Referee takes control of the PC for one (in-game) hour, during which the creature will rampage wildly and without mercy.

In addition, **during combat** the werewolf character must make a Wis check each time it deals or takes damage or be under the control of the Referee during the subsequent round. After such a Referee-controlled round, the player will have one round to do as they please before they must go back to making Wis checks each round. The werewolf will attempt to eat anything slain by its own hand and will fight anyone who gets in its way.

Witch Sisters Three

FIRST CAME THORN, THEN FROST, THEN CAME BLACK-HAIRED DREAD—the youngest of the three oldest witches in the world, an illusionist and deceiver. Her familiar is the crow called **Ear Eater**. She travels the Devoured Land disguised as a servant to Prince Nygnengeth, of whom she has *devised a crude talking hex-golem*, accompanied by some huntsmen. She traffics in the arts of fear.

Dread

HD 20 **HP** 100 **Speed** 120'

Armor 12 **Morale** 11

Attack

† **Knife**: +6 to hit d4hp and, once the knife is in, it reduces a target's saves by 5 and can be used to deliver touch spells. Removing the knife without washing the wound in holy water causes 2d10hp.

† **Spells** used in combat typically include (each at least once daily, see Spell section for descriptions, pg 112): *Nightmare Frenzy, Spontaneous Amputation, Drown in Ashes, Domain of Decay, Caress into Oblivion, Paranoia, Spell Epidemic, Hand of Doom, Wheels of Confusion*, and the standard spells *Darkness* and *Heal*.

Attack/Defense

Dread has a 10' *Cause Fear* aura.

Defense

† Any **damage inflicted on Dread is also inflicted on the attacker/caster** so long as Ear Eater lives. This also includes status effects such as stunning or *Confusion*, though not *Charm* or *Suggestion*-type effects which allow the caster to elicit specific actions.

† Dread **will never appear to lose hit points** or be hurt or affected in any way until Ear Eater is dead. You can't save your way past this illusion but inconsistencies in her behavior arising from status effects might tip foes off.

† *Heal* (2/day).

Special

† Dread has access to the spells a 20th lvl Cleric and Magic-User would. She can perform any cosmetically spooky and thematically appropriate magical effect you can think of, given a few rounds of peace—like she could cut herself, let her blood run out in a circle on the ground and turn the circle into a portal to somewhere else.

† Dread can **use Ear Eater's senses**—see though her eyes, hear through her ears, etc., they can communicate as one mind.

† **Language of Scales**: All Witches can read the skins of serpents.

Ear Eater

HD 8 **HP** 40 **Speed** 240'

Armor 16 (high Dex)

Morale 11

Attack

† **Eye gouge**: +6 or autohit on a helpless victim, 2d6hp and victim is blinded in one eye. Victim must make a Con check each morning to restore sight, failing 3 times in a row means the eye is permanently useless. Also: three successful gouges on the same target means the eye has been removed.

† **Ear gouge**: +6 to hit 2d6hp and victim is deaf in one ear. Victim must make a Con check each morning to restore hearing, failing 3 times in a row means the ear is permanently useless.

† **Quadruple damage** on a sneak attack.

Defense

† Crows are **allied to death**. They cannot be harmed by those who have never killed another of their same species.

† Ear Eater **regenerates** 10hp per round until reduced to zero.

Special

† **Sleight of hand** (pick pocket small items, sever cords, etc.) 5 in 6.

† **Stealth** 5 in 6.

False Prince and Huntsmen (Hex Golems)

THIS ANIMATE EFFIGY only looks and acts like a prince while its mistress smiles. Otherwise it looks like some fucked mud-stick thing with peach pit eyes. The huntsmen are more gruesome yet.

HD 1 **HP** 8 **Speed** 120'

Armor 16

Morale 12

Attack

† **Grapple**: +1 to hit, 12 Str

† **Nibble**: +1 to hit d4hp. Delivers a knot of worms (see Worms) onto the target.

frost

FROST IS THE MIDDLE SISTER of three witches as old as the Devoured Lands and lives in the center of Gutgloaming Lake with her owl, Tormentor. White-haired, blue-lipped, she claims dominion over snow and cold and frigid things. While waiting for her sisters to arrive and help her end the world, she makes pies out of different kinds of babies.

HD 20 **HP** 100 **SPEED** 120'

ARMOR 12

MORALE 11

ATTACK

† **Knife**: +6 to hit d4hp and, once the knife is in, it reduces a target's saves by 5 and can be used to deliver touch spells. Removing the knife without washing the wound in holy water causes 2d10hp.

† **Spells** used in combat typically include (each at least once daily, see Spell section for descriptions pg 112): *Blizzard Beasts, Cold Winds of Funeral Dust, Frozen by Icewinds, Frostdemonstorm, Arctic Swarm, Snowblind, Spell Epidemic* and the standard spells *Gust of Wind, Wall of Ice,* and *Heal.*

ATTACK/DEFENSE

† When angered, Frost has an **aura of cold** that extends 10' around her in every direction. It automatically inflicts d10hp on anything inside it and freezes any opposing spell that is not fire or heat-based that hits it (heat-based spells have half-normal effect). Enemy spells hit the edge of the aura and fall to the ground in the form of softball-sized crystals. These can be picked up and hurled up to 20' at (and by) anyone, and, when they hit an appropriate target, will shatter and take effect normally as if the thrower were the caster. The aura also coats the ground in an ice slick, causing all within it to save vs Paralysis or fall each round. The aura also coats weapons as well—anyone making a melee attack with a weapon must make an additional save not to drop it.

DEFENSE

† Frost is **blind** but so long as Tormentor lives, she can see normally.

† *Heal* (2/day)

SPECIAL

† Frost has access to the spells a 20th lvl Cleric and Magic-User would. She can perform any cosmetically spooky and thematically appropriate magical effect you can think of, given a few rounds of peace—like she could throw her head back, blow a spit bubble, have it freeze, pull it out and hand it to you with a frozen spell inside.

† Frost **can use Tormentor's senses**—see though her eyes, hear through her ears, etc., they can communicate as one mind.

† **Language of Scales**: All Witches can read the skins of serpents.

Tormentor

Tormentor targets Clerics first, then Magic-Users.

HD 4 **HP** 20 **SPEED** 240'

ARMOR 15 (high Dex)

MORALE 11

ATTACKS (2 attacks per round)

† **Claw**: +6 to hit d6hp

† If both claw attack succeed in the same round on a spellcaster, Tormentor will then attempt to **rip their tongue out**— save vs Breath Weapon or take 2d6hp and lose your tongue.

† Automatically **steals a word** (see Owls) when encounter begins.

DEFENSE

† Tormentor may **save twice** vs Magic and take the better save.

† Tormentor is allowed a **save even against magic offering no save**.

SPECIAL

† Tormentor has a permanent *True Seeing* effect on at all times.

Thorn

THORN IS A WITCH, THE ELDEST of her three sisters, her hair is grey, and longer than her arms. She is a friend to growing, creeping things, she rides on the back of the wolf, Lair Abbess. She will offer parties enchanted food, to turn them into animals. If they refuse she will become impatient and attempt to destroy them.

HD 20 **HP** 100 **SPEED** 120'

ARMOR 12

MORALE 11

ATTACK

† **Knife**: +6 to hit d4hp and, once the knife is in, it reduces a target's saves by 5 and can be used to deliver touch spells. Removing the knife without washing the wound in holy water causes 2d10hp.

† **Spells** used in combat typically include (each at least once daily, see Spell section for descriptions pg 112): *Web of Thorns*, *Internal Stoats*, *Reanimate Dead Wood*, *Feast of Claws*, *Poison Eye*, *Fruits of Stupidity*, *Spell Epidemic*, *Sweet Leaf*, and the standard spell *Heal*.

DEFENSE

† So long as Lair Abbess lives, Thorn is **immune to ordinary physical attacks and weapons** (even magic weapons).

† Thorn wears **7 unholy symbols** around her neck, each granting the ability to counter one of the 7 levels of Cleric magic. The counter sends an unholy version of the spell back at the caster.

SPECIAL

† Thorn has access to the spells a 20th lvl Cleric and Magic-User would. She always has *Insect Plague*, *Find the Path*, *Lose the Path*, *Faerie Fire*, *Howl of the Moon*, *Plant Growth*, *Speak with Animals*, and *Speak with Plants* prepared and has basically any cosmetically spooky and thematically appropriate spell effect you can think of, given a few rounds of peace—like she could, for instance, cut her fingernails off, put them in a mash, eat the mash and grow fangs.

† Thorn **can use Lair Abbess' senses**—see though her eyes, hear through her ears, etc., they can communicate as one mind.

† **Language of Scales**: All Witches can read the skins of serpents.

Lair Abbess

HD 7 **HP** 35 **SPEED** 180'

ARMOR 14

MORALE 11

ATTACKS (2 attacks per round)

† **Bite** +7 to hit 2d8+3hp

DEFENSE

† Any edged weapon doing half its full possible damage or less (i.e. if a weapon does d8, then 4 or less) becomes **lodged in Lair Abbess' body** and cannot be moved until the next sunrise.

† Lair Abbess may **save twice vs Magic** and take the better save.

† Lair Abbess is allowed a **save even against magic offering no save**.

SPECIAL

† Anyone seeing a wolf must **drink a toast** to it the following night—or more will come.

Wolves

THE WOLF IS WRATHFUL, despising humankind in particular—and dogs, whom they see as willing slaves. The wolves of the Devoured Land are, quite simply, the most efficient killers the Referee can possibly create—they seek not victory, nor even food, but murders. They are loathe to disengage without having winnowed the opposing pack by at least one. They will ambush, drive enemies downhill or toward water, risk everything until they make the first kill and immediately flee thereafter if the tide of the hunt goes against them. Anyone seeing a wolf must drink a toast to it the following night—or more will come.

Typical wolf

HD 3 **HP** 15 **SPEED** 180'

ARMOR 14

MORALE 11 (Wolves never check morale until at least one foe is dead)

ATTACK

† *Bite* +3 to hit 2d4hp

SPECIAL

† Anyone seeing a wolf must **drink a toast** to it the following night—or more will come.

Ditch Mother

DITCH MOTHER favors the pincer attack. 2d4 of her pack appear at first, then 2d4 appear from the opposing direction the next round. Her lair is an ice cave, strewn with bones, the shriveled hearts of the dead, and whatever indigestible wealth these meals wore.

HD 7 **HP** 35 **SPEED** 180'

ARMOR 14

MORALE 12 (Wolves never check morale until at least one foe is dead)

ATTACKS (2 attacks per round)

† *Bite* +7 to hit 2d8+1hp

† Ditch Mother's *gaze* acts as a *Cause Fear* spell.

DEFENSE

† *Immune to magic.*

SPECIAL

† Ditch Mother can **sense the presence** and location of any creature that walks across her tracks in the snow, no matter how far away.

† Anyone seeing a wolf must drink a toast to it the following night—or more will come.

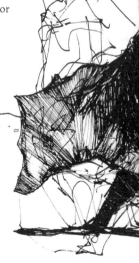

Skintaster

Is ALLIED TO THE CROW, Vorvik. The crows scout for wealthy parties by air and harry them, then steal from the dead after the wolves come.

HD 5 **HP** 20 **SPEED** 180'

ARMOR 14

MORALE 12 (Wolves never check morale until at least one foe is dead)

ATTACK

† *Bite* +5 to hit 2d6+1hp

SPECIAL

† Anyone seeing a wolf must ***drink a toast*** to it the following night—or more will come.

Cromlech

Longs TO EAT Jex Amon of the Frostbitten Moons, who scarred her face 3 years ago—and to eat her dogs as well. You'll do, though.

HD 5 **HP** 20 **SPEED** 180'

ARMOR 14

MORALE 12 (Wolves never check morale until at least one foe is dead)

ATTACK

† *Bite* +5 to hit 2d6+1hp

SPECIAL

† Anyone seeing a wolf must ***drink a toast*** to it the following night—or more will come.

Lair Abbess

Is FAMILIAR TO THE WITCH, Thorn, and is listed alongside her.

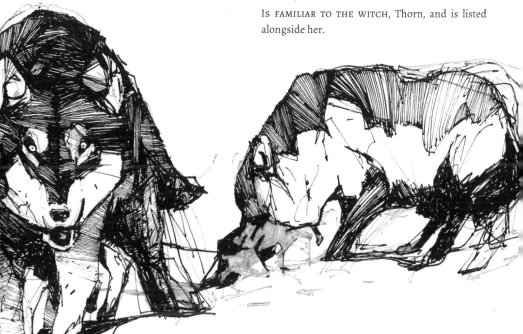

Worms

WORMS WILL WAIT, THEY ARE SLOTHFUL. They can afford to be, for in the end all shall fall and feed their wet, worming faces. They don't travel much. In the Devoured Lands, they can still grow by spontaneous generation—in rations of any kind. That's generally what a random encounter result of "worms" indicates.

They share one mind, however, and can be bargained with, should that occur to the party stumbling upon a knot of them and managing to speak to them. Make their lives easier and they will gladly grant surcease from dining on the party's packs or wounds.

Knot of Worms

HD 2–6 **HP** 8–24 **SPEED**
NEGLIGIBLE ARMOR 10
MORALE 3
ATTACK
† **Bite**: +2-6 to hit (as HD) save vs Poison or contract Worm Rot.
SPECIAL
† If a foe touches anything with a knot of worms on it or in it, this counts as an **automatic hit** for the bite attack.

Worm Rot

THE MOST COMMON illness carried by worms of the Devoured Land, it has an *incubation period* of 2 hours (i.e. take damage after 2 hours), an *interval* of 24 hours (i.e. save again every 24 hours or take damage) and a *duration* equal to (20 minus the victim's Con) days (i.e. the infection ends after that many days). Each failed save causes **d4 hit points** of damage and **vomiting**.

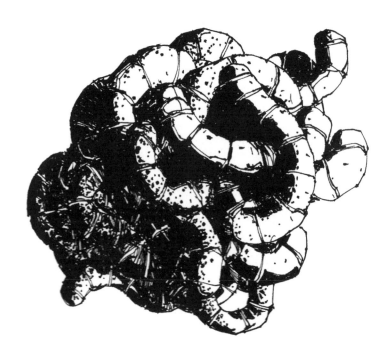

Calendar and MAP

THERE IS A SERIES of events unfolding behind the cold and austere facade of the Devoured Land. Referees interested in a structured campaign should intrigue to inveigle their players in these machinations. Perhaps they are sought as allies by one party or another, perhaps they are sent to investigate disturbances, perhaps a powerful patron sees an opportunity to gain arcane knowledge from the witches. Read through the scenario and have fun thinking of ways the party might intersect with it.

No matter when they left wherever they came from, the party will arrive on the map at the second day of the second month—the 28 Days of the Purifier. This isn't simple railroading—it is always the Days of the Purifier in the Devoured Land. The area does not currently respect the proper sequence of time in the outer world.

The reason is this:

The three witches, Thorn, Frost, and Dread, seek to unleash a demon—Belphegor the Beast—so that he might lay waste to this earth, and incarnate the ruin of all that now is. The ceremony can only be performed once every thousand years, on the twenty-fourth day of the second month—the festival of Dragobete—and only in the Dim Fortress, whose whereabouts are unknown.

The witches searched for this place and could not find it, and so in the dying light of the final day they cast a spell, a spell that turned the hourglass of the Devoured Lands back to the second day of the second month, the day called Fastelavn, and time ran forward again.

Creatures not present during the original run of these days may enter (when they arrive *it will always be the 2nd Day of the Purifier*) and leave the remote Devoured Land as usual, but those that were run the sequence from the second to the 24th day of the second month repeatedly without knowing it.

The charm is this: unless Belphegor is summoned or Ratatoskr, the Slandering Marmot, fails to see his shadow on Fastelavn, the days from the 2nd to the 24th will repeat, forever.

The nihilistic witches' only hope is that some interloper will inadvertently alter the sequence of events that prevents them from finding the Dim Fortress before Dragobete.

Events

THE MAP AND KEY given here represent the situation in each area as of the first time the players come upon it. Assuming the players do nothing to alter them, the following events will occur (and if they stay past the 24th, they will see them recur again):

2ND *(New Moon)* **DAY OF THE PURIFIER:** The Amazon tribes wear whalebone masks in observance of Fastelavn. Ratatoskr sees his shadow.

3RD *(Waxing Crescent Moon)* Mad Maggot Queen Rindr finds the rat called Ribboned Jenny. Bartering for her freedom with the mad queen, Jenny reveals that she knows Prince Nygnengeth of Nornrik is hunting in the Devoured Land.

4TH *(Waxing Crescent Moon)* Sam the Moth and Garvik Nerves of the Arsonists have an argument. After two days of searching, Nerves wants to find the secret entrance to the Dim Fortress, Sam wants easier prey. Sam leaves.

5TH *(Waxing Crescent Moon)* Stryx the owl sees Ratatoskr emerge from a secret entrance to the Dim Fortress, bringing gossip to the trolls of Lachrymose Peak.

6TH *(Waxing Crescent Moon)* Sam the Moth is captured by the Peak trolls while trying to steal their gold.

7TH *(Waxing Crescent Moon)* Frostbitten Moons have a large but indecisive battle with the Ulvenbrigad. The Moons begin to wonder why the Ulvenbrigad are so far north.

8TH *(First Quarter Moon)* Sam escapes.

9TH *(Waxing Gibbous Moon)* Sam sees the witch Dread's retinue, disguised as Prince Nygnengeth's, consulting the trolls.

10TH *(Waxing Gibbous Moon)* The owl Stryx meets up with Tormentor, familiar of the witch called Frost, tells her about the secret entrance to the Dim Fortress.

11TH *(Waxing Gibbous Moon)* Garvik Nerves offers a deal to Black Sky, Nerves will give them half the treasure from the Dim Fortress if they protect the Arsonists until they find an entrance.

12TH *(Waxing Gibbous Moon)* Maggot Sisters capture Sam who offers to lead the Sisters to the "Prince" in exchange for her freedom.

13TH *(Waxing Gibbous Moon)* The Maggots capture the "Prince" and his "cook". Sam, tired of being captured, returns to Nerves.

14TH *(Full Moon)* Rindr and Dread come to an agreement—the Maggot Sisters will protect the three witches as they enter the Dim Fortress.

15TH *(Waning Gibbous Moon)* The Thirteen capture a Maggot Sister and discover Rindr's plan.

16TH *(Waning Gibbous Moon)* The Thirteen battle a werewolf, take casualties.

17TH *(Waning Gibbous Moon)* A group of the Ulvenbrigad capture some of the remaining Thirteen, including Malicia Orgen.

18TH *(Waning Gibbous Moon)* The Frostbitten Moons defeat the main force of the Ulvenbrigad. The captured Thirteen flee.

19TH *(Waning Gibbous Moon)* The Frostbitten Moons search for and round up the fleeing Thirteen.

20TH *(Waning Gibbous Moon)* The Thirteen reveal to the Moons that they've learned of the Maggot Sisters' plans to aid the witches entering the Dim Fortress.

21ST *(Waning Gibbous Moon)* A war party of the Frostbitten Moons attacks and is defeated by the Maggot Sisterhood, however, a Cold Banner assassin manages to infiltrate the Sisterhood's ranks.

22ND *(Third Quarter Moon)* Rindr and the three witches—Thorn, Frost, and Dread—meet at Gutgloaming Lake (G8). Frost agrees to lead them to the entrance of the Dim Fortress, which she has learned about from Tormentor.

23RD *(Waning Crescent Moon)* The witches and a host of Maggots head north toward the mountain.

24TH *(Waning Crescent Moon)* The festival of Dragobete. Late that night, the host approaches the Arsonists' camp. Cold Banner assassin slays Queen Rindr, the Arsonists take advantage of the disarray to attack, the witches summon Stryx's parliament of owls to defend them from the crows. The witches eventually drive off the Arsonists but by then it's too late to enter the mountain.

The Months

INCIDENTALLY, THE MONTHS, as the Amazons know them are:

1. January—Days of the Second Head
2. February—Days of the Purifier
3. March—Days of Slaying
4. April—Days of the Threshold (Rivers unfreeze)
5. May—Days of the Withering
6. June—Days of the Quickening
7. July—Days of the Drinker of Tears
8. August—Days of the Betrayed
9. September—Days of the Chronically Ill
10. October—Days of the Octopus and the Squid (Rivers freeze)
11. November—Days of the Rainsnout
12. December—Days of The Fat

The Map

THE MAP ON THE NEXT PAGE lists one feature for every 6x6-mile area—feel free to add as many more as you like. If the party is simply passing through it (two hours travel on foot, one on horseback), they may not notice it unless it's something big, like a castle. If they search the area (this takes four hours), they'll find it. Remember you can see three miles over flat ground, more if you're on a mountain. Roll an encounter every two hours (see **Encounters**). Everything in bold print has a separate entry in this book. Remember all bodies of water are frozen from the Days of the Octopus and Squid (October) to the Days of the Threshold (April).

The party is most likely to enter the Devoured Lands along the road from Rottingkroner (Area 7H—but it should be transposed with 6A if the campaign is set in historical Norway), but any area works, and they may may travel in all eight directions.

Tumbledown inn overrun by wharf **rats** in search of **Ribboned Jenny**, a fancy-rat from **Rottingkroner** (see H5).

Note: each area measures 6x6 miles.

A small case in red frogskin lying in the dirt harbors a love potion and a candle whose light exposes fae, false, invisible and magical things.

Shifting winds have revealed a princess voluntarily encased in ice for one thousand three hundred years. On her twentieth birthday, court seers had informed the unkillable girl that she was cursed to slay the next person she laid eyes upon—and she decided she would rather not. If freed, she'll immediately flee but improbably cross paths with her liberator with Jennifer-Aniston-movie-esque frequency forever thereafter. Actually, she isn't going to kill anyone—the prophecy was just wrong. It turns out the entrails for "repeatedly run through" and "repeatedly run into" are gratingly similar.

A pack **goat** named Sprogsmal trundles across the plain, its mistress, a poet, long dead. Its saddlebags contain poems worth 3000sp to anyone with a large purse and a respect for quality literature.

Fourteen children ages 6-12. Armed and averse to adult supervision. They'll probably be eaten soon. One has a random **Witch Spell** on a scroll which she will read if threatened.

Cave walls dense with nested and discoesque cubes of pyrite reflect not the present but the future selves of the PCs. Two encounter checks worth of study will reveal enough details of future dangers and opportunities—the observer is +2 to saves until the next level-up—or the Referee may offer the player a fortune from the table in *Vornheim: The Complete City Kit* should he or she have access to that remarkable and indispensable tome.

A murder of **crows** under **Black Sky** scavenge a wolf kill in a shallow valley—a luckless neophyte of the Maggot Sisterhood. They snatch at both her jewelry (150sp worth) and the branded skin beneath.

The main force of the Amazons of the **Ulvenbrigad** is here, in hilltop earthworks that twist like an intestinal tract, overlooking the "trap town" of Thridi. **Choard**, the sacred bastard, wallows feverishly in a rockpiled redoubt at the center of the hill and the approaches are thick with scarred sentinels and guard **wolves**.

Mauthlic Gaunt is, one hopes, some kind of anthropologist. At any rate, he has a trunk full of dolls and effigies gathered from across the continent. If the party tells him about the snow man in Eelhome, he will pay them 1000sp to take him safely to it, and will reward them with 1000sp more upon arrival out of sheer joy.

A party member will feel their foot snap through a membrane stretched like drumleather just beneath the snow's surface. This turns out to be the wing of a vast pale dead ancient winged reptile the size of a god, stretched between bones thick as ash trunks. A Magic-User examining this skin for two weeks will gain a level—providing they can read the language of **serpent** skins.

A hilltop ring of simple graves like outsize molars, interlaced with mutilated **Ulvenbrigad** slain in an ambush by the **Frostbitten Moons**. One has the *Whispering Panic* spell tattooed on her left arm.

The Spitter is a foreign scholar monk who sits contemplating the mountains and the nature of truth. Using medieval standards for both, pick a distant land and a sexual impropriety. He hails from the first and has been exiled for the second. The Spitter is fond of hiking, eager to trade information and sworn to eschew violence. He is evil if you like.

Low slanting walls of larvikite slab form the home of Pleasant Lora the alewidow, who brews a storied bock. Rare visitors have bartered a wide enough variety of durable goods in exchange for this lager that her home is now about as close as the western Devoured gets to a trading post. Her hearth is warm and her inventory is fairly random.

A large and unusually cryophilic plum tree is home to Ratatoskr, the Slandering Marmot.

Lord Amozark (Lvl 6 Fighter) and three lieutenant constables have tracked the **Arsonists** (in Area 2F) to the Devoured Land from **Rottingkroner**. He is attempting to bring them in for the murder of one Aarstein Oyseth and will mistake the players' characters for the patchwork band of heavily-armed eccentrics he seeks.

The small, remote settlement known as Thridi has light in the windows and hogs in the pens. These lie—Thridi was raided months ago by the **Ulvenbrigad**, and this show of shelter and warmth is used to entrap ignorant animals and travelers to relieve them of their meat and valuables, respectively.

A surveyor lies dead. **Worms** crawl into him and then out again. His notebook contains a sketch of the location of the tower of the **Cold Banner** (unlabeled) (see E1), a drawing of a skeleton in a moldy jerkin, and the names of 2 **drowning demons**.

Pearlholders have nailed a pair of lovers to either side of a yew, inverted, with three large nails outside one of their churches. One stake through their trunks and the tree's, two more through the backs of their hands, nailed knuckle to knuckle. One woman is dead, the other will be soon. Her dying wish is vengeance. Their crime was never explained.

A bridge above the lair of two **trolls**, **Gruntling** and The Fibbing Troll, provides the only access to the oozing volcanic caldera of Lachrymose Peak. Manheim the clown (see E8) is among the many luckless souls still alive in the Fibbing Troll's Effigy Net. There is also a scroll with a random Witch Spell on one of the dead victims.

A tongue of ice, 200' tall and 5' wide tumbles from one distributary of the Slith down into another. Climbing this frozen waterfall offers a secret entrance to the trolls' lair at **Lachrymose Peak**. From the Days of the Threshold (April) until the Days of the Rainsnout (November) the route thaws and this route is inaccessible.

The large black sessile oaks that twist their way across the lower altitudes are particularly thick here. An encounter roll of 21-30 indicates an ambush by creatures of the Referee's choice.

This wood is the territory of **Transcending Massacre** and her drift of 16 **snow leopards**.

The witch called **Thorn** passes through the wood riding her wolf, **Lair Abbess** on her way to meet her sisters in G8. She will be offended if fellow travelers refuse her gifts of lutefisk and doghead pie, which are, of course, poisoned and will turn them into lemmings.

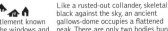

Like a rusted-out collander, skeletal black against the sky, an ancient gallows-dome occupies a flattened peak. There are only two bodies hung from the vaulting woodwork, a useless surgeon and the author of a despicable crab pudding, both installed by the **Ulvenbrigad** in an extending web of their own entrails through which small animals creep to feast on their remains.

Mammoth skulls and the smell of butchered geese announce the southernmost rim of the territory of the **Frostbitten Moons**. These **Amazons** dwell in the dead batteries and outworks of a lost castle or fortified city. Approaching from leeward, the party will see the leaning and snow-covered ruin-homes striped in bright yellow with luminous paint.

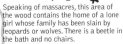

Mist like clotted milk. A failed (passive) Bushcraft roll brings the party out in an adjacent area other than the one they intended.

Two old men walk along a bridge of whitewood and bog iron bisecting the Slith. Neither knows the other is a disguised immortal. They are Onthryn Star-Eater, Lord of botulism and whales and Vystrid Innyrthronde. They discuss politics and the sea.

A parliament of **owls** nests here, ruled by **Stryx**. Their vocabulary is growing. If the party has already had an owl encounter but has not summoned them, they will only hear them hooting.

Prince Nygngeneth of **Nornrik** and eight huntsmen seek the Narthex Hart, a legendary stag whose antlers respectively map and reflect the route of the Slith and its river system. It does not exist. They are Fighters of whatever level you prefer.

Speaking of massacres, this area of the wood contains the home of a lone girl whose family has been slain by leopards or wolves. There is a beetle in the bath and no chairs.

On the edge of the forest lies **Sevenfold Tower**, containing seven temptations, seven curses and seven treasures.

A small black ceramic jar in an abandoned watermill contains a vial of poison and a scroll inscribed with the *Chain of Skin* spell.

A machicolated tower set into a section of otherwise demolished face wall is home to the assassins of the **Cold Banner**—a secret sect of the **Frostbitten Moons**. Their training and meditation rooms are home to a wide variety of data about targets—physical, social, geographical, and astrological.

A clutch of 14 stoppered forest glass orbs have gathered at a narrow bend against the north bank of the river. These are the ashes of dead children of the **Frostbitten Moon** clan, stymied by the tide on their way down the Slith to the Halls of the Fallen. The **Frostbitten Moons** will be in the party's debt if they are returned and will launch them again at the spring equinox. Any witch will pay 300sp per orb, which they will use to make terrible monsters.

The **Dim Fortress** lies, sunken and concealed, beneath the peak of Mount Hellebor. Amid many perils and dangers, **Nidhoggr** lies imprisoned within, sucking the bodies of the piled dead. Only the Slandering Marmot, **Ratatoskr** (B6) knows the way inside.

Describe the large and cloudlike mounds of snow at the base of the mountain. If this doesn't clue the party in to how **avalanche**-prone this area is, maybe a passive Bushcraft check will.

Three **Ulvenbrigad** heading to the Garden of Emptiness (F3).

A pile of eyes lies here, tall as a horse, each impaled on a bodkin. It is unclear to whom this message is intended or from whom it emanates, though presumably they know—their friends having returned from whatever they were doing with far fewer eyes or bodkins than they left with.

Two performing dwarfs—Ordo, a tumbler, and Chao, a juggler—are the new occupants of a squat sentry turret carved from the rockside, hung with wolfskin and loaded with snares, provisions, and crossbow bolts. They search the Devoured Land for their companion—a clown named Manheim (see C3).

Largely useless, the tiny trading post known as Eelhome is remarkable for two reasons: it is home to a competent physician (Int 16) and to a massive anthropomorphic snow effigy with tree branches in place of arms—its purpose unknown. The snow statue is decorated with vegetables and sagging hessian.

Behind a frozen waterfall the party will find three covered pit traps filled with sharpened icicles. Behind that, they'll find the lair of **The Arsonists**—they are looking for the secret entrance to the **Dim Fortress**.

The eastern slope of Mount Hellebor is known to the **Amazons** as the Garden of Emptiness not because of the 200' chasms that rend the rock, but for the unusually efficient and painless strains of abortifacient herbs (kvann and, of course, hellebore) that grow in them. An encounter roll of 21-24 indicates d4+1 **Frostbitten Moons** come to gather herbs for their decoctions, 25-26 indicates **Maggot Sisters** here for the same purpose, 27-28 indicates **Ulvenbrigad**, 29-30 **The Thirteen**.

Dominating this area is the great round bowl of The Swallowing, a glacial Lake ringed by 10' of flat path and bouldered slopes in every direction, thus giving the party a choice of venues in which to be attacked by **drowning demons**—out on the lake itself, on the narrow path, or while climbing.

A coffin-sized stone plinth is smeared in something small and dead. The **Ulvenbrigad** left this offering—they claim the yellow-eyed wolf that rules this area from an overgrown chain of low, barrel-like towers is a lycanthrope. This is entirely accurate. A Bushcraft roll will reveal the **werewolf's** territory is crisscrossed with human and animal tracks but is disturbingly devoid of territorial marking.

A severed tongue rests on the north bank of the river.

A thin blue powder is marbled into the snow on the north bank of the Slith. Collecting it (with gloves) will yield two doses of **Forgetting Dust**, collecting it without gloves will yield confused adventurers.

A stone monument carved with the Sign of the She-Goat is hammered into the semifrost. A message in an ancient dialect of the **Amazons** reads "Here lie the honorably and dishonorably fallen of the Battle of The Immense Treachery". Digging beneath will reveal 4500sp worth of coins and grave goods spread across hundreds of graves—all of it cursed.

What the **Maggot Sisters** left of this adventuring party the worms are now finishing—except they missed a 2000sp tube with a *Drunk's Reversal* scroll hidden in a wizard's sleeve.

Prince Nygnengeth of Nornrik, accompanied by his aging cook and 6 retainers, heads toward **Rottingkroner** to hunt with a vassal lord. Except his cook is not his cook—she is the witch, **Dread**, the prince is a false **prince** made of sea salt and pitch, and the huntsmen are filled with worms. Dread's crow—**Ear Eater**—wheels high above.

Freeze-and-thaw cycles have cracked this land into a series of pinnacles, linked occasionally by natural ice bridges. Treat encounter rolls of 21-30 as an **owl** encounter (by day) or **crows** (by night).

Anyone paying close attention to their dog or making a successful Bushcraft roll will notice a large amount of scent marking in this area—signaling the domain of a pack of 36 tundra **wolves** lead by **Ditch Mother**.

A spidering of pink lichen and a **dead** goat.

An abandoned fortress sinks into a high crag, flooded by its own moat. The knee-deep waters inside contain strange rays and misshaped ratfish—and 6000sp worth of pearls in a water-sealed box.

An arctic **fox** named Orthening Weeve creeps across the subtundra, seeking the rat known as **Ribboned Jenny** (H5). She is high-born and considered a delicacy.

What appears at first to be a barren white tree emerging at an angle from the center of a small island in the Slith is actually the tibia of a dead **giant** from the **Hatemountain**. The "island" is formed from congealed fat and things that collected in it. A charm to render crawling creatures immobile for six seconds is carved into the bone; it works once.

Gutgloaming Lake is interrupted by a spit of crooked land, the tip of which houses a rime-laced tower attached to half a bridge. The white witch **Frost** dwells within, and an owl known as **Tormentor** roosts above, the witch house is strange and includes books that will teach 7 random **Witch Spells**. The angelfish in the lake grow to be as big as bats.

A rimless wheel reaches from the white ground like a failed hand, marking the resting place of a doomed merchant caravan. Successful Bushcraft will reveal the footprints leading away from the dead merchants and slain fjord horses belong to a pack of **snow leopards** (led by **Unfolding-And-Immanent-Mercy**). Searching the area long enough to trigger an encounter check will turn up 600sp plus the remains of a cunningly-wrought leopard cage made of **ektesvarsk** worth 1800sp that lies just beneath the snow.

Limbless and malformed creatures dead of exposure or starvation surround a translucent pool of viscid aqua that reshapes whatsoever it touches. Mutant carnivores frequent this **Misshaping Pool** to feed on the damned.

Hexagonal terraces of packed ice built against the mountainside form the redoubt where the **Maggot Sisterhood** have made camp with their spitz-hounds and warswine. Their mad maggot queen **Rindr**, surrounded by concubines, is searching for **Nidhoggr**—from whom she seeks some incomprehensible and no doubt blasphemous accommodation.

The Thirteen ride stolen draft horses and spy on the **Maggot Sisters**. Their leader, eight-eyed **Malicia Orgen**, is wondering what mad queen **Rindr** is up to. They'll sell you drugs.

Five crates rest on a cliff edge high above the sled that pulled them. One contains salted cod, one contains 650sp worth of aquavit, one contains an occult text with the names of 4 drowning demons and a map to the entrance to the **Dim Fortress**, one contains a sleeping **snow leopard**, one contains beets and **Ribboned Jenny** the champion **rat**. Her swarm is nearby.

A fallen clone of **King Ovv** lies broken on the ice, holding a sword of **Ektesvarsk** and bleeding a substance like caramelized agate. Herbs found only on Mount Hellebor cling to his sackcloth hem. Harmless.

The road from **Rottingkroner** ends here in a field of accumulated surface hoar and scree. This is a relatively safe area and a successful Bushcraft roll will easily turn up an ermine or game bird worth eating. There is a statue of St. Ælfheah—credited with converting the first Christian king—holding an axe here, though his stone head has been replaced with that of a stylized she-goat.

Duke Dethelredd (Lvl 7 Fighter) was sent to the lonely fortress of Vryngirslott with 67 mercenaries to nominally "defend" the nominal "frontier" from witches and Amazons as a punishment for some obscure insult to his liege lord. They will join travelers for a melancholy meal of fish porridge and shallow-poached brill before hurrying them back out into the snow.

Locations

THIS SECTION REPEATS the area descriptions from the map on the previous page. Regardless of shape on the map, each area measures 6 miles across.

A1

TUMBLEDOWN INN overrun by wharf rats in search of Ribboned Jenny, a fancy-rat from Rottingkroner (see H5).

A2

A SMALL CASE in red frogskin lying in the dirt harbors a love potion and a candle whose light exposes fae, false, invisible and magical things.

A3

SHIFTING WINDS have revealed a princess voluntarily encased in ice for one thousand three hundred years. On her twentieth birthday, court seers had informed the unkillable girl that she was cursed to slay the next person she laid eyes upon—and she decided she would rather not. If freed, she'll immediately flee but improbably cross paths with her liberator with Jennifer-Aniston-movie-esque frequency forever thereafter. Actually, she isn't going to kill anyone—the prophecy was just wrong. It turns out the entrails for "repeatedly run through" and "repeatedly run into" are gratingly similar.

A4

A PACK GOAT NAMED Sprogsmal trundles across the plain, its mistress, a poet, long dead. Its saddlebags contain poems worth 3000sp to anyone with a large purse and a respect for quality literature.

A5

FOURTEEN CHILDREN ages 6-12. Armed and averse to adult supervision. They'll probably be eaten soon. One has a random Witch Spell on a scroll which she will read if threatened.

A6

CAVE WALLS DENSE with nested and discoesque cubes of pyrite reflect not the present but the future selves of the PCs. Two encounter checks worth of study will reveal enough details of accessory and scar to grant insight into future dangers and opportunities—the observer is +2 to saves until the next level-up—or the Referee may offer the player a fortune from the table in *Vornheim: The Complete City Kit* should he or she have access to that remarkable and indispensable tome.

A7

A MURDER OF CROWS under Black Sky scavenge a wolf kill in a shallow valley—a luckless neophyte of the Maggot Sisterhood. They snatch at both her jewelry (150sp worth) and the branded skin beneath.

A8

THE MAIN FORCE of the Amazons of the Ulvenbrigad is here, in hilltop earthworks that twist like an intestinal tract, overlooking the "trap town" of Thridi. Choard, the sacred bastard, wallows feverishly in a rockpiled redoubt at the center of the hill and the approaches are thick with scarred sentinels and guard wolves.

B1

MAUTHLIC GAUNT is, one hopes, some kind of anthropologist. At any rate, he has a trunk full of dolls and effigies gathered from across the continent. If the party tells him about the snow man in Eelhome, he will pay them 1000sp to take him safely to it, and will reward them with 1000sp more upon arrival out of sheer joy.

B2

A PARTY MEMBER will feel their foot snap through a membrane stretched like drumleather just beneath the snow's surface. This turns out to be the wing of a vast pale dead ancient winged reptile the size of a god, stretched between bones thick as ash trunks. A Magic-User examining this skin for two weeks will gain a level—providing they can read the language of serpent skins.

B3

A HILLTOP RING of simple graves like outsize molars, interlaced with mutilated Ulvenbrigad slain in an ambush by the Frostbitten Moons. One has the Whispering Panic spell stabbily tattooed on her left arm.

B4

THE SPITTER IS A FOREIGN scholar monk who sits contemplating the mountains and the nature of truth. Using medieval standards for both, pick a distant land and a sexual impropriety. He hails from the first and has been exiled for the second. The Spitter is fond of hiking, eager to trade information and sworn to eschew violence. He is evil if you like.

B5

LOW SLANTING WALLS of larvikite slab form the home of Pleasant Lora the alewidow, who brews a storied bock. Rare visitors have bartered a wide enough variety of durable goods in exchange for this lager that her home is now about as close as the western Devoured gets to a trading post. Her hearth is warm and her inventory is fairly random.

B6

A LARGE AND UNUSUALLY cryophilic plum tree is home to Ratatoskr, the Slandering Marmot.

B7

LORD AMOZARK (Lvl 6 Fighter) and three lieutenant constables have tracked the Arsonists (in Area 2F) to the Devoured Land from Rottingkroner. He is attempting to bring them in for the murder of one Aarstein Oyseth and will mistake the players' characters for the patchwork band of heavily-armed eccentrics he seeks.

B8

THE SMALL, REMOTE SETTLEMENT known as Thridi has light in the windows and hogs in the pens. These lie—Thridi was raided months ago by the Ulvenbrigad, and this show of shelter and warmth is used to entrap ignorant animals and travelers to relieve them of their meat and valuables, respectively.

C1

A SURVEYOR LIES DEAD. Worms crawl into him and then out again. His notebook contains a sketch of the location of the tower of the Cold Banner (unlabeled) (see E1), a drawing of a skeleton in a moldy jerkin, and the names of 2 drowning demons.

C2

PEARLHOLDERS have nailed a pair of lovers to either side of a yew, inverted, with three large nails outside one of their churches. One stake through their trunks and the tree's, two more through the backs of their hands, nailed knuckle to knuckle. One woman is dead, the other will be soon. Her dying wish is vengeance. Their crime was never explained.

C3

A BRIDGE ABOVE THE LAIR of two trolls, Gruntling and The Fibbing Troll, provides the only access to the oozing volcanic caldera of Lachrymose Peak. Manheim the clown (see E8) is among the many luckless souls still alive in the Fibbing Troll's Effigy Net. There is also a scroll with a random Witch Spell on one of the dead victims.

C4

A TONGUE OF ICE, 200' tall and 5' wide tumbles from one distributary of the Slith down into another. Climbing this frozen waterfall offers a secret entrance to the trolls' lair at Lachrymose Peak. From the Days of the Threshold (April) until the Days of the Rainsnout (November) the route thaws and this route is inaccessible.

C5

THE LARGE BLACK sessile oaks that twist their way across the lower altitudes are particularly thick here. An encounter roll of 21-30 indicates an ambush by creatures of the Referee's choice.

C6

THIS WOOD IS the territory of Transcending Massacre and her drift of 16 snow leopards.

C7

THE WITCH CALLED Thorn passes through the wood riding her wolf, Lair Abbess on her way to meet her sisters in G8. She will be offended if fellow travelers refuse her gifts of lutefisk and doghead pie, which are, of course, poisoned and will turn them into lemmings.

C8

LIKE A RUSTED-OUT COLLANDER, skeletal black against the sky, an ancient gallows-dome occupies a flattened peak. There are only two bodies hung from the vaulting woodwork, a useless surgeon and the author of a despicable crab pudding, both installed by the Ulvenbrigad in an extending web of their own entrails through which small animals creep to feast on their remains.

D1

MAMMOTH SKULLS and the smell of butchered geese announce the southernmost rim of the territory of the Frostbitten Moons. These Amazons dwell in the dead batteries and outworks of a lost castle or fortified city. Approaching from leeward, the party will see the leaning and snow-covered ruin-homes striped in bright yellow with luminous paint.

D2

MIST LIKE CLOTTED milk. A failed (passive) Bushcraft roll brings the party out in an adjacent area other than the one they intended.

D3

TWO OLD MEN WALK along a bridge of whitewood and bog iron bisecting the Slith. Neither knows the other is a disguised immortal. They are Onthryn Star-Eater, Lord of botulism and whales and Vystrid Innyrthronde, Maker of all Claws. They discuss politics and the sea.

D4

A PARLIAMENT of owls nests here, ruled by Stryx. Their vocabulary is growing. If the party has already had an owl encounter but has not summoned them, they will only hear them hooting.

D5

PRINCE NYGNENGETH of Nornrik and eight huntsmen seek the Narthex Hart, a legendary stag whose antlers respectively map and reflect the route of the Slith and its river system. It does not exist. They are Fighters of whatever level you prefer.

D6

SPEAKING OF MASSACRES, this area of the wood contains the home of a lone girl whose family has been slain by leopards or wolves. There is a beetle in the bath and no chairs.

D7

ON THE EDGE of the forest lies the Sevenfold Tower, containing seven temptations, seven curses and seven treasures.

D8

A SMALL BLACK ceramic jar in an abandoned watermill contains a vial of poison and a scroll inscribed with the *Chain of Skin* spell.

E1

A MACHICOLATED TOWER set into a section of otherwise demolished face wall is home to the assassins of the Cold Banner—a secret sect of the Frostbitten Moons. Their training and meditation rooms are home to a wide variety of data about targets—physical, social, geographical, and astrological.

E2

A CLUTCH OF 14 stoppered forest glass orbs have gathered at a narrow bend against the north bank of the river. These are the ashes of dead children of the Frostbitten Moon clan, stymied by the tide on their way down the Slith to the Halls of the Fallen. The Frostbitten Moons will be in the party's debt if they are returned and will launch them again at the spring equinox. Any witch will pay 300sp per orb, which they will use to make terrible monsters.

E3

THE DIM FORTRESS lies, sunken and concealed, beneath the peak of Mount Hellebor. Amid many perils and dangers, Nidhoggr lies imprisoned within, sucking the bodies of the piled dead. Only the Slandering Marmot, Ratatoskr (B6), knows the way inside.

E4

DESCRIBE THE LARGE and cloud-like mounds of snow at the base of the mountain. If this doesn't clue the party in to how avalanche-prone this area is, maybe a passive Bushcraft check will.

E5

A SEVERED TONGUE rests on the north bank of the river.

E6

THREE ULVENBRIGAD heading to the Garden of Emptiness (F3).

E7

A PILE OF EYES lies here, tall as a horse, each impaled on a bodkin. It is unclear to whom this message is intended or from whom it emanates, though presumably they know—their friends having returned from whatever they were doing with far fewer eyes or bodkins than they left with.

E8

TWO PERFORMING DWARFS—Ordo, a tumbler, and Chao, a juggler—are the new occupants of a squat sentry turret carved from the rockside, hung with wolfskin and loaded with snares, provisions, and crossbow bolts. They search the Devoured Land for their companion—a clown named Manheim (see C3).

F1

LARGELY USELESS, the tiny trading post known as Eelhome is remarkable for two reasons: it is home to a competent physician (Int 16) and to a massive anthropomorphic snow effigy with tree branches in place of arms—its purpose unknown. The snow statue is decorated with vegetables and sagging hessian.

F2

BEHIND A FROZEN waterfall the party will find three covered pit traps filled with sharpened icicles. Behind that, they'll find the lair of The Arsonists—they are looking for the secret entrance to the Dim Fortress.

F3

THE EASTERN SLOPE of Mount Hellebor is known to the Amazons as the Garden of Emptiness not because of the 200' chasms that rend the rock, but for the unusually efficient and painless strains of abortifacient herbs (kvann and, of course, hellebore) that grow in them. An encounter roll of 21-24 indicates d4+1 Frostbitten Moons come to gather herbs for their decoctions, 25-26 indicates Maggot Sisters here for the same purpose, 27-28 indicates Ulvenbrigad, 29-30 The Thirteen.

F4

DOMINATING THIS AREA is the great round bowl of The Swallowing, a glacial Lake ringed by 10' of flat path and bouldered slopes in every direction, thus giving the party a choice of venues in which to be attacked by drowning demons—out on the lake itself, on the narrow path, or while climbing.

F5

A coffin-sized stone plinth is smeared in something small and dead. The Ulvenbrigad left this offering—they claim the yellow-eyed wolf that rules this area from an overgrown chain of low, barrel-like towers is a lycanthrope. This is entirely accurate. A Bushcraft roll will reveal the werewolf's territory is crisscrossed with human and animal tracks but is disturbingly devoid of territorial marking.

F6

A thin blue powder is marbled into the snow on the north bank of the Slith. Collecting it (with gloves) will yield two doses of Forgetting Dust, collecting it without gloves will yield confused adventurers.

F7

A stone monument carved with the Sign of the She-Goat is hammered into the semifrost. A message in an ancient dialect of the Amazons reads "Here lie the honorably and dishonorably fallen of the Battle of The Immense Treachery". Digging beneath will reveal 4500sp worth of coins and grave goods spread across hundreds of graves—all of it cursed.

F8

What the Maggot Sisters left of this adventuring party the worms are now finishing—except they missed a 2000sp tube with a Drunk's Reversal scroll hidden in a wizard's sleeve.

G1

Prince Nygnengeth of Nornrik, accompanied by his aging cook and 6 retainers, heads toward Rottingkroner to hunt with a vassal lord. Except his cook is not his cook—she is the witch, Dread, the prince is a false prince made of sea salt and pitch, and the huntsmen are filled with worms. Dread's crow—Ear Eater—wheels high above.

G2

Freeze-and-thaw cycles have cracked this land into a series of pinnacles, linked occasionally by natural ice bridges. Treat encounter rolls of 21-30 as an owl encounter (by day) or crows (by night).

G3

Anyone paying close attention to their dog or making a successful Bushcraft roll will notice a large amount of scent marking in this area—signaling the domain of a pack of 36 tundra wolves lead by Ditch Mother.

G4

A spidering of pink lichen and a dead goat.

G5

An abandoned fortress sinks into a high crag, flooded by its own moat. The knee-deep waters inside contain strange rays and misshaped ratfish—and 6000sp worth of pearls in a water-sealed box.

G6

An arctic fox named Orthening Weeve creeps across the subtundra, seeking the rat known as Ribboned Jenny (H5). She is high-born and considered a delicacy.

G7

What appears at first to be a barren white tree emerging at an angle from the center of a small island in the Slith is actually the tibia of a dead giant from the Hatemountain. The "island" is formed from congealed fat and things that collected in it. A charm to render crawling creatures immobile for six seconds is carved into the bone; it works once.

G8

GUTGLOAMING LAKE is interrupted by a spit of crooked land, the tip of which houses a rime-laced tower attached to half a bridge. The white witch Frost dwells within, and an owl known as Tormentor roosts above, the witch house is strange and includes books that will teach 7 random Witch Spells. The angelfish in the lake grow to be as big as bats.

H1

A RIMLESS WHEEL reaches from the white ground like a failed hand, marking the resting place of a doomed merchant caravan. Successful Bushcraft will reveal the footprints leading away from the dead merchants and slain fjord horses belong to a pack of snow leopards (led by Unfolding-And-Immanent-Mercy). Searching the area long enough to trigger an encounter check will turn up 600sp plus the remains of a cunningly-wrought leopard cage made of ektesvarsk worth 1800sp that lies just beneath the snow.

H2

LIMBLESS AND MALFORMED creatures dead of exposure or starvation surround a translucent pool of viscid aqua that reshapes whatsoever it touches. Mutant carnivores frequent this **Misshaping Pool** to feed on the damned—see Misshaped Animals (pg 47) and Deformations of the Misshaping Pool (pg 133).

H3

HEXAGONAL TERRACES of packed ice built against the mountainside form the redoubt where the Maggot Sisterhood have made camp with their spitz-hounds and warswine. Their mad maggot queen Rindr, surrounded by concubines, is searching for Nidhoggr—from whom she seeks some incomprehensible and no doubt blasphemous accommodation.

H4

THE THIRTEEN RIDE stolen draft horses and spy on the Maggot Sisters. Their leader, eight-eyed Malicia Orgen, is wondering what mad queen Rindr is up to. They'll sell you drugs.

H5

FIVE CRATES REST on a cliff edge high above the sled that pulled them. One contains salted cod, one contains 650sp worth of aquavit, one contains an occult text with the names of 4 drowning demons and a map to the entrance to the Dim Fortress, one contains a sleeping snow leopard, one contains beets and Ribboned Jenny the champion rat. Her swarm is nearby.

H6

A FALLEN CLONE of King Ovv lies broken on the ice, holding a sword of Ektesvarsk and bleeding a substance like caramelized agate. Herbs found only on Mount Hellebor cling to his sackcloth hem. Harmless.

H7

THE ROAD FROM Rottingkroner ends here in a field of accumulated surface hoar and scree. This is a relatively safe area and a successful Bushcraft roll will easily turn up an ermine or game bird worth eating. There is a statue of St. Ælfheah—credited with converting the first Christian king—holding an axe here, though his stone head has been replaced with that of a stylized she-goat.

H8

DUKE DETHELREDD (Lvl 7 Fighter) was sent to the lonely fortress of Vryngirslott with 67 mercenaries to nominally "defend" the nominal "frontier" from witches and Amazons as a punishment for some obscure insult to his liege lord. They will join travelers for a melancholy meal of fish porridge and shallow-poached brill before hurrying them back out into the snow.

The Dim Fortress

(in location E3)

CAN ONLY BE REACHED via a narrow cave mouth deep in the crenellations of Mount Hellebor. Unless Ratatoskr or some other creature is being followed to the entrance, the only way to discover it for the first time is to make three successful Search rolls in a row (assume a maximum of 4 such rolls may be made in a given day). The cave mouth leads to an erratic and dark chimney-like shaft reaching 238' feet, past hopelessly caved-in sections of fortress terminating at last in a stone door, its locks long ago rusted off, leaving a hole big enough for a marmot to squeeze through.

Much of the original Dim Fortress has been annihilated by time and geology, but the areas here represent what is still accessible. Assume ceilings are 100' high unless drawn onto the map. The walls are made of black stone carved with scenes of primordial myth nearly abraded into abstraction. There are no doors except where drawn in on the map and there is no light. Remember to describe only what the party can see via the light available to them.

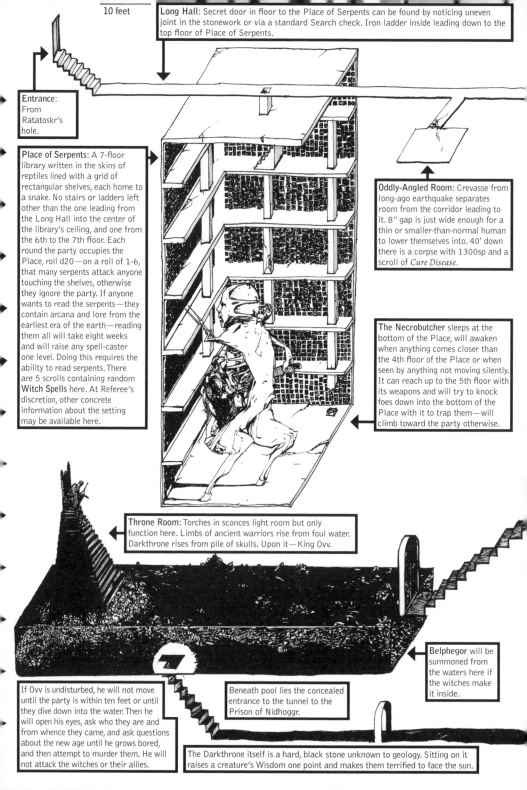

10 feet

Long Hall: Secret door in floor to the Place of Serpents can be found by noticing uneven joint in the stonework or via a standard Search check. Iron ladder inside leading down to the top floor of Place of Serpents.

Entrance: From Ratatoskr's hole.

Place of Serpents: A 7-floor library written in the skins of reptiles lined with a grid of rectangular shelves, each home to a snake. No stairs or ladders left other than the one leading from the Long Hall into the center of the library's ceiling, and one from the 6th to the 7th floor. Each round the party occupies the Place, roll d20—on a roll of 1-6, that many serpents attack anyone touching the shelves, otherwise they ignore the party. If anyone wants to read the serpents—they contain arcana and lore from the earliest era of the earth—reading them all will take eight weeks and will raise any spell-caster one level. Doing this requires the ability to read serpents. There are 5 scrolls containing random **Witch Spells** here. At Referee's discretion, other concrete information about the setting may be available here.

Oddly-Angled Room: Crevasse from long-ago earthquake separates room from the corridor leading to it. 8″ gap is just wide enough for a thin or smaller-than-normal human to lower themselves into. 40' down there is a corpse with 1300sp and a scroll of *Cure Disease*.

The Necrobutcher sleeps at the bottom of the Place, will awaken when anything comes closer than the 4th floor of the Place or when seen by anything not moving silently. It can reach up to the 5th floor with its weapons and will try to knock foes down into the bottom of the Place with it to trap them—will climb toward the party otherwise.

Throne Room: Torches in sconces light room but only function here. Limbs of ancient warriors rise from foul water. Darkthrone rises from pile of skulls. Upon it—King Ovv.

Belphegor will be summoned from the waters here if the witches make it inside.

If Ovv is undisturbed, he will not move until the party is within ten feet or until they dive down into the water. Then he will open his eyes, ask who they are and from whence they came, and ask questions about the new age until he grows bored, and then attempt to murder them. He will not attack the witches or their allies.

Beneath pool lies the concealed entrance to the tunnel to the Prison of Nidhoggr.

The Darkthrone itself is a hard, black stone unknown to geology. Sitting on it raises a creature's Wisdom one point and makes them terrified to face the sun.

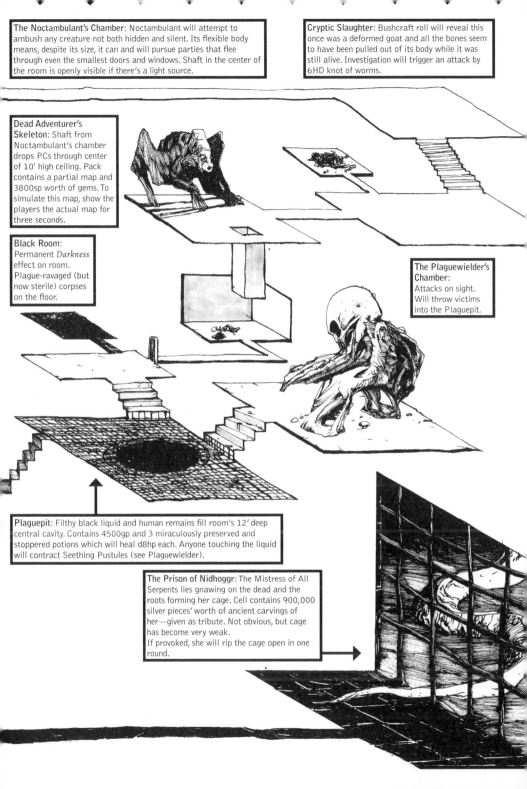

The Noctambulant's Chamber: Noctambulant will attempt to ambush any creature not both hidden and silent. Its flexible body means, despite its size, it can and will pursue parties that flee through even the smallest doors and windows. Shaft in the center of the room is openly visible if there's a light source.

Cryptic Slaughter: Bushcraft roll will reveal this once was a deformed goat and all the bones seem to have been pulled out of its body while it was still alive. Investigation will trigger an attack by 6HD knot of worms.

Dead Adventurer's Skeleton: Shaft from Noctambulant's chamber drops PCs through center of 10' high ceiling. Pack contains a partial map and 3800sp worth of gems. To simulate this map, show the players the actual map for three seconds.

Black Room: Permanent *Darkness* effect on room. Plague-ravaged (but now sterile) corpses on the floor.

The Plaguewielder's Chamber: Attacks on sight. Will throw victims into the Plaguepit.

Plaguepit: Filthy black liquid and human remains fill room's 12' deep central cavity. Contains 4500gp and 3 miraculously preserved and stoppered potions which will heal d8hp each. Anyone touching the liquid will contract Seething Pustules (see Plaguewielder).

The Prison of Nidhoggr: The Mistress of All Serpents lies gnawing on the dead and the roots forming her cage. Cell contains 900,000 silver pieces' worth of ancient carvings of her—given as tribute. Not obvious, but cage has become very weak.
If provoked, she will rip the cage open in one round.

Locations

THIS SECTION REPEATS the room descriptions from the Dark Fortress map on the previous page.

Entrance

FROM RATATOSKR's hole.

Long Hall

SECRET DOOR in floor to the Place of Serpents can be found by noticing uneven joint in the stonework or via a standard Search check. Iron ladder inside leading down to the top floor of Place of Serpents.

Place of Serpents

A 7-FLOOR LIBRARY written in the skins of reptiles lined with a grid of rectangular shelves, each home to a snake. No stairs or ladders left other than the one leading from the Long Hall into the center of the library's ceiling, and one from the 6th to the 7th floor. Each round the party occupies the Place, roll d20—on a roll of 1-6, that many serpents attack anyone touching the shelves, otherwise they ignore the party. If anyone wants to read the serpents—they contain arcana and lore from the earliest era of the earth—reading them all will take eight weeks and will raise any spell-caster one level. Doing this requires the ability to read serpents. There are 5 scrolls containing random Witch Spells here. At Referee's discretion, other concrete information about the setting may be available here.

The Necrobutcher sleeps at the bottom of the Place, will awaken when anything comes closer than the 4th floor of the Place or when seen by anything not moving silently. It can reach up to the 5th floor with its weapons and will try to knock foes down into the bottom of the Place with it to trap them—will climb toward the party otherwise.

Oddly-Angled Room

CREVASSE FROM long-ago earthquake separates room from the corridor leading to it. 8" gap is just wide enough for a thin or smaller-than-normal human to lower themselves into. 40' down there is a corpse with 1300sp and a scroll of *Cure Disease*.

Cryptic Slaughter

BUSHCRAFT ROLl will reveal this once was a deformed goat and all the bones seem to have been pulled out of its body while it was still alive. Investigation will trigger an attack by 6HD knot of worms.

The Noctambulant's Chamber

NOCTAMBULANT will attempt to ambush any creature not both hidden and silent. Its flexible body means, despite its size, it can and will pursue parties that flee through even the smallest doors and windows. Shaft in the center of the room is openly visible if there's a light source.

Dead Adventurer's Skeleton

SHAFT FROM Noctambulant's chamber drops PCs through center of 10' high ceiling. Pack contains a partial map and 3800sp worth of gems. To simulate this map, show the players the actual map for three seconds.

Black Room

PERMANENT *Darkness* effect on room. Plague-ravaged (but now sterile) corpses on the floor.

Plaguepit

FILTHY BLACK liquid and human remains fill room's 12' deep central cavity. Contains 4500gp and 3 miraculously preserved and stoppered potions which will heal d8hp each. Anyone touching the liquid will contract Seething Pustules (see Plaguewielder).

The Plaguewielder's Chamber

ATTACKS ON SIGHT. Will throw victims into the Plaguepit.

Throne Room

TORCHES IN SCONCES light room but only function here. Limbs of ancient warriors rise from foul water. Darkthrone rises from pile of skulls. Upon it—King Ovv.

If Ovv is undisturbed, he will not move until the party is within ten feet or until they dive down into the water. Then he will open his eyes, ask who they are and from whence they came, and ask questions about the new age until he grows bored, and then attempt to murder them. He will not attack the witches or their allies.

The Darkthrone itself is a hard, black stone unknown to geology. Sitting on it raises a creature's Wisdom one point and makes them terrified to face the sun.

Beneath pool lies the concealed entrance to the tunnel to the Prison of Nidhoggr.

Belphegor will be summoned from the waters here if the witches make it inside.

The Prison of Nidhoggr

THE MISTRESS of All Serpents lies gnawing on the dead and the roots forming her cage. Cell contains 900,000 silver pieces' worth of ancient carvings of her—given as tribute. Not obvious, but cage has become very weak.

If provoked, she will rip the cage open in one round.

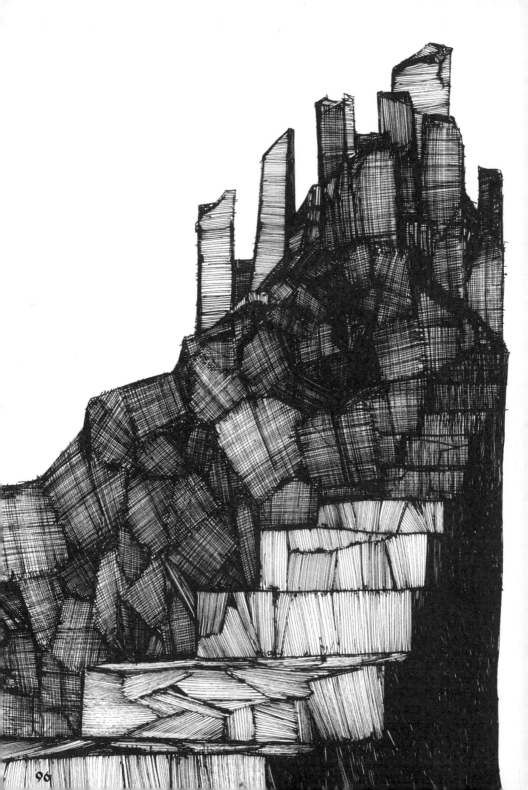

Sevenfold Tower

(in location D7)

THE TOWER APPEARS from the outside to be abandoned but relatively intact, with impressive double doors.

Running the Sevenfold Tower requires forcibly splitting the party and then paying careful attention to when you "cut" from one PC to the next and how much information each player has. It involves a series of "tests" that the players should not know are tests. Feel free to vary the cosmetic details of the tests, especially if you have more than four players and so have to repeat them. The main point (other than to conceal the nature of the tests) is to try to make it always seem like a PC you aren't talking to might be in mortal danger. Read through the entire scenario before running it so you can get a handle on how it works.

Before running this, label your players' PC's secretly. The player to your left has "First PC", the player to their left has "Second PC", the player to your right has "Last PC". If there are more players, they are "Middle PCs".

Use the map (next page) that matches the number of PCs you have.

Ideally, all of the characters will enter the tower quickly. If not, describe some winding unlit stone corridors, with various arbitrary lefts and rights until they do enter. If some still wait outside, describe an immense and ornate door, untouched for centuries, unlocked. The ceilings are 10' high, the walls are invulnerable, the corridors are well-lit by torches in sconces.

As soon as the entire party is inside—or the door is opened—describe a wave of black engulfing everyone, they feel disoriented.

Roll lots of dice, look up often, at each player, as if checking things. Ask for their Search skills, Spell saves, Wisdom scores, current hit points. Look concerned or amused, write things down.

NOW ROLL FOR REAL then pretend to pick a random PC—pick the First PC. They appear alone at "First PC Start", continue until the PC makes a decision about the Lust Test, then move to the second PC, continue until the 2nd PC has made a decision about the Wrath or Gluttony Test (whichever they encounter first), then move to the 3rd PC etc. etc. until all the PCs have made a decision about at least one test, then start again with the First PC and Referee them until they make a decision about another test or meet another PC, then continue around the table. Keep going until all living PCs have met up.

AT SOME POINTS a creature will "leap from the shadows"—this will turn out to be an NPC adventurer gone mad, near death. They have 1hp and +0 to hit with a pathetic weapon for 1hp of damage. They appear just to provide a cliffhanger moment and make it believable that they might be in danger.

VAGUE SHRIEKS in the distance, likely from other PCs. The PC feels themselves disoriented, screaming, missing an arbitrary percent of their hit points (this may seem unfair, don't worry, the hit points aren't really lost, it just seems that way). Make each room seem cosmetically different and make it seem like the character has been in a fight they can't remember.

Lust Test:

AT THE T-JUNCTION the PC will clearly perceive two things: to the left, approximately 60' away, a lost and slightly scuffed and confused version of the most attractive possible individual (or individuals) from the First PC's point of view (though do not use those words—the player will sense something is up—imagine the PC's perfect mate and describe them in neutral terms) who quickly ducks around the corner. To the right, the bloodied, damaged personal effects of the Second PC with a blood trail leading away. Second PC can't act yet, just ask First PC what they want to do.

If First PC goes toward the attractive stranger, secretly write "GOAT" next to their name in your notes. The attractive NPC(s) seem pleasantly surprised to see someone else. Either way, tell the player they see a sudden movement leap at them from the shadows, then, unless all the PCs have met up, go "Ok, let's move on to...(next PC)".

Gluttony Test:

ANOTHER T JUNCTION as above. Left: approximately 60' away, a dead adventurer—a stranger—their pack is open and rations and healing potions (say whatever will make it clear there are healing potions) spills out. Right: Desperate screams of another PC (or an innocent child if all PCs have been found), with a blood trail leading away.

If PC goes toward the food and potions, write "PIG" next to their name. The stuff is real, there are d4 potions that heal d4hp each, the rations are enough for a day. Either way, tell the player they see a sudden movement leap at them from the shadows, then, unless all the PCs have met up, go

ANOTHER T JUNCTION as above. Left: approximately 60' away, a small, very weak-looking Trollkin (tiny troll—stats as dog). It aggressively mocks the PC in the most irritating and offensive way the Referee can, within the bounds of friendship with his or her players, and immediately ducks around the corner. Right: Screams of another PC (one who hasn't been addressed yet or who has been attacked by a "shadow") or a child (if no PC is plausibly available).

If PC chases after the troll, write "WOLF" next to their name. Either way, unless all the PCs have met up, go "Ok, let's move on to...(next PC)".

Greed Test:

ANOTHER T JUNCTION as above. Left: about 60' away, an obviously dead Amazon—her spilled pack is filled with glittering gems. Right: Screams of another PC (one who hasn't been addressed yet or who has been attacked by a "shadow") or a child (if no PC is plausibly available), with a blood trail leading away.

If they go toward the dead Amazon, she springs to life (well, undeath) and attacks with her axe (stats as Typical Ulvenbrigad Amazon, except undead), write "CROW" next to their name. Either way, unless all the PCs have met up, go "Ok, let's move on to...(next PC)".

WHEN ALL THE PCs have met up (and, if there are 3 PCs, after at least one has encountered the Gluttony Test) ...a previously overlooked door behind them will open, revealing an ornate room full of polished black gems and silver. An aged crone with a crown of antlers will step forward saying: "You would escape this tower? There is one challenge left. Who is the greatest among you? Who will face the challenge?" No one will be able to move or take any action except discuss who will go. The crone will only repeat this question. If anyone volunteers themselves right off the bat, mark "STAG" next to their name. Either way, let the party decide. Once it is decided, the crone will say "Very well, you shall be the champion, and the reward shall be yours. Is this acceptable to you?" Pause. If any of the party members go "Aw man, I didn't know there was a reward..." secretly mark "RAT" next to their

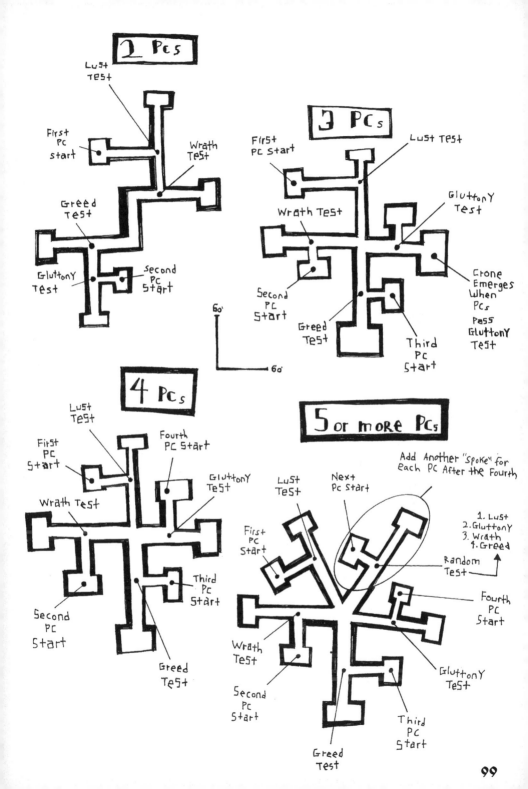

2 PCs

Lust Test
First PC start
Wrath Test
Greed Test
Gluttony Test
Second PC Start

3 PCs

First PC Start
Lust Test
Wrath Test
Gluttony Test
Crone Emerges When PCs Pass Gluttony Test
Second PC Start
Greed Test
Third PC Start

60'
60'

4 PCs

Lust Test
Fourth PC Start
First PC Start
Gluttony Test
Wrath Test
Second PC Start
Third PC Start
Greed Test

5 or more PCs

Add Another "Spoke" for Each PC After the Fourth

Lust Test
Next PC start
First PC Start
1. Lust
2. Gluttony
3. Wrath
4. Greed
Random Test
Fourth PC Start
Wrath Test
Second PC Start
Gluttony Test
Third PC Start
Greed Test

99

THE CHALLENGE

WHOEVER IS EVENTUALLY chosen will be allowed to step into the gem-filled room (assume it's 60' x 60'). There they will battle an Ulvenbrigad warrior or witch with exactly the same stats, level, etc. as themselves. The equipment may be different, but will be mechanically the same. If the PC wins, the Crone will open an entrance in the wall. If the PC loses, they die, and the Crone re-issues the challenge and a new champion must be chosen, on and on until they are all dead or someone wins.

AS THEY LEAVE, she will speak as follows:

† If any PC has "PIG" next to their name she will say that they have been gluttonous (for the healing potions) and placed their need over the well-being of their comrades. That PC becomes a **pig** instantly.

† If any PC has "WOLF" next to their name, she will say they have been wrathful (toward the trollkin) and placed their rage over the well-being of their comrades. That PC becomes a **wolf** instantly.

† If any PC has "STAG" next to their name, she will say they have been prideful (about being the greatest) and placed their self-love above the well-being of their comrades. That PC becomes a **stag** instantly.

† If any PC has "RAT" next to their name, she will say they have been envious (about not getting the champion's reward) of their comrades. That PC becomes a **rat** instantly.

† If any PC has "GOAT" next to their name, she will say they have been lustful (about the hottie(s) they saw) and placed their desires above the well-being of their comrades. That PC becomes a **goat** instantly.

† If any PC has "CROW" next to their name, she will say they have been greedy (about the gems) and placed their need for wealth above the well-being of their comrades. They become a **crow** instantly.

† If any PC had a time where they didn't do anything and instead kinda bummed around doing nothing or doing something irrelevant while hearing their friends in trouble, she will say they have been slothful. They become a **worm** instantly.

† If a PC was guilty of more than one sin, she will make them into an **appalling hybrid** of the appropriate animals.

† If any PC escaped sin, she will give them an **ornate vial** of holy water worth 2000sp.

† If no-one did any of these things, the crone will tell them they have been noble, always putting their friends (and maybe innocent children) before self, flesh, hate, hunger, covetousness, want, or inertia and give them **all the gems** in the room, totaling 18,000sp or 3000 per party member, whichever is higher, in addition to the ornate vials mentioned above.

† If players attack the crone, she will be revealed to be spectral, intangible, and immune to harm or any kind.

TELL ANY PLAYER that got turned into an animal that they'll get 2000xp for playing in character as soon as they find a way to turn themselves back to human. To undo these transformations, see "Breaking Curses, pg 132—any witch will know the steps to take.

Character classes, spells, substances, and survival skills

Amazon Warriors
as player characters

REFEREES MAY WISH to make Amazons available as player characters. In an ongoing campaign, I suggest making this option "unlock" as soon as a player loses a PC in the Devoured Land. In the Lamentations of the Flame Princess system, at first level, the Amazon has the following stats:

HP: 1d8
TO HIT: +1

AN AMAZON IS SIMILAR to a Fighter, however instead of a steadily increasing to-hit bonus, the Amazon rolls twice on the table on pg 104 each time they level up. The consequence of rolling the same result twice is indicated. Maximum bonus to anything is +10.

(If you're using another system, just start the Amazon as a first level Fighter with a to-hit bonus that's one less than usual, then follow the rest of these instructions.)

IN ADDITION, Amazon Warriors pick a clan and get an attendant benefit:

† **Frostbitten Moons** start with 4 doses of contact poison—to which specific poison they are immune—the target takes 2 hit points of damage per round until they save vs Poison. In addition, the Amazon character is presumed to be able to manufacture a new dose once a month.

† **Maggot Sisters** start play with a trained warpig (see boar) or may roll an extra time on the table below.

† **Ulvenbrigad** start play with a trained wolf.

† Members of **The Thirteen** start play with 4 doses of Witherbound powder, see *New Substances* section (pg 118) for effects.

Members of other clans which you invented roll once on the Amazon Warrior traits table (next page), unless the player and Referee want to hack together some other benefit. Which I encourage. Make something cool, like a clan that has bat-sonar or something.

| | | | | Saving throws | | | |
Level	Experience	HP	Paralyze	Poison	Breath	Device	Magic
1	0	1d8	14	11	14	15	16
2	2,000	+1d8	14	11	14	15	16
3	4,000	+1d8	14	11	14	15	16
4	8,000	+1d8	12	9	12	13	14
5	16,000	+1d8	12	9	12	13	14
6	32,000	+1d8	12	9	12	13	14
7	64,000	+1d8	10	7	8	11	12
8	128,000	+1d8	10	7	8	11	12
9	256,000	+1d8	10	7	8	11	12
10	384,000	+3*	8	5	6	9	10
11	512,000	+3*	8	5	6	9	10
12	640,000	+3*	8	5	6	9	10
13+	+128,000/lvl	+3*	6	3	4	7	8

*Constitution modifiers no longer apply

Ò100 Amazon Warrior traits

AN AMAZON LEVELS UP when a Fighter would (i.e. 2nd level at 2000xp, 3rd level at 4000xp, etc.). Whenever an Amazon levels up, add d8hp (plus any Con modifier) and rolls twice on this table. The consequence of rolling the same result twice is indicated. Maximum bonus to anything is +10.

1-29 +1 to hit.

30-45 +1 to any three of your saves.

46 You have a second attack per round. You divide your usual attack bonus however you like between opponents/strikes. You get another extra attack per round every time you re-roll this result.

47-48 +1 Con up to racial max. Numbers in excess go to Str or Dex.

49-50 If a creature more than 10' tall knocks you down to half or fewer hit points, you may summon your fury to inflict triple damage on a hit. This only works once per opponent. Unless you re-roll this result, then it works twice, or three times, etc. etc.

51-53 You now have a 2 in 6 Bushcraft skill. Add one point each time this is re-rolled.

54 Quest: that thing you wanted? The Jewel of Carmathroq? The Map to the Pleasure Pits of Mazuun? The Spiked Club of Ooolatt? It's there. Four sessions worth of adventure away or less. Tell your Referee, who then must place it.

You must have a fair shot at it—like any other treasure, but there's no guarantee you will get it. If you don't get it by the fourth session you can keep trying or let it go and roll again on this table. However, if you choose to roll again and then you do get the thing somehow anyway, you lose whatever gimmick you rolled. Referee, think up some clever reason why.

55-56 You can intimidate hostile beasts of animal intelligence into accepting you as dominant so long as nobody in your party has attacked them. Basically, roll d10 and add your charisma or level (whichever is higher) and the Referee rolls d10 + the creature's meanness, rated on a scale of 1-20 by the Referee with 20 being like some mother bear that just watched you eat all her baby bear's heads and is also mind-controlled by a hostile witch doctor. If the "Charisma attack" works, the creature will calm down. If the charm offensive fails, you are effectively at unarmored, flat-footed armor rating

the next round because you are really not scaring them there and are walking right up to the animal. Good luck with that. If you re-roll this result while leveling up, take +1 to hit or all saves.

57 You are totally used to tromping around in the wilderness. In any wooded environment (or whatever other one you are a native of) you cannot be surprised and will always notice anyone coming at least 2 rounds away unless they are actively planning an ambush. Your experience with the landscape and the way it grows allows you to search a wilderness hex at twice the ordinary speed and if you are pursuing or being pursued through the wilderness you add your level, in feet, to your relative speed for purposes of determining who catches who. If you re-roll this, the expertise extends to all outdoor environments, re-roll again and it goes for dungeons, re-roll again and cities, again and it works in like the planes, re-roll again and you should probably just re-roll on this table until you get something different.

58 +1 Str up to racial max. Numbers in excess go to Con or Dex.

59-60 You may take half an hour out of your busy schedule and eat the heart of an animal that you and your party (of 10 or fewer people) killed (a regular, non-magical animal, though prehistoric animals and maybe some other weird monsters count at the Referee's discretion). You yourself must have delivered the killing blow. After you do that, you gain the offensive strength of that creature for one hour (# of attacks, bonus to attack, damage) but are also kind of nuts and cannot speak except in short grunts (you can point). You can preserve the heart for as long as you want before doing this. Do this more than once per day and you will go completely crazy. Re-roll this result and the effect lasts an extra hour.

61 +1 damage. If you roll this again it jumps to +3, then +5, +7, etc.

62-63 +2 vs toxins, poisons, and whatever other saves might be considered derivable from your general good health in the system you're using. +3 vs inebriation. Same bonuses again each time you re-roll this.

64-65 On a melee hit you can do your usual damage plus knock a human-sized opponent back 10. If you try it twice on the same opponent they get a Str check against you (d10 + whole Str vs d10 + whole Str). If you roll this result again you get 2 free shoves before the opposed checks kick in. After that, re-roll.

66 On a melee hit you can do your usual damage plus knock a human-sized opponent of equal HD or less prone. If you try it twice on the same opponent they get a save or Str check or something against you. If you roll this result again on this table, you get 2 free knockdowns before the saves kick in, then 4. After that, re-roll.

67 You are now +2 to hit in two of the following situations: from horseback, in unarmed combat, or with a bow or crossbow. Your choice. If you eventually roll all of those and keep re-rolling this result, you start getting +2 to weird fighting situations you can make up, like fighting blind or on fire or whatever, subject to Referee approval blah blah blah

68-69 +2 to checks to intimidate people, -1 to charm or lie to fancy folk. +2 more to intimidate when you re-roll this thereafter.

70-71 A single hit that normally would have killed you just maims you instead. You lose an arm below the elbow or leg below the knee, your choice. If you re-roll this you can "bank" another one or, if you've already lost a limb, the next time you get magically healed it comes back. **72-73** Your crit range extends by one. Now you do double damage on a 19 or 20. Keep rolling this and it keeps extending.

74-75 Your knowledge of the natural world gives you a sense of the unnatural. You can detect the presence (but not the precise location) of ghostly or invisible things on a 1 in 6. Goes up by one each time you roll this result

76-79 So long as you have 1 hit point, you gain d4hp from taking a drink of any strong spirit. However, with each drink after the first in an hour, you must make a successful Wis check to hit the right target when attacking. Re-rolling this result increases your tolerance—it will be 3 drinks before you must make a Wis check, then four, then five, etc.

80-82 You have "Frazetta armor". You may add your Cha bonus and Str bonus to your armor rating when not wearing armor. If you have no Cha or Str bonus then you're a loser but treat this roll as if you just upped your Cha by one. Re-rolling this means your Cha goes up by one, until there's a bonus.

83-84 You do d6 + Str bonus damage unarmed. You go up one die each time you re-roll this.

85-86 On a successful hit you can hold anything whose Str and Dex are both less than your Str for an extra round automatically before it starts to get checks to escape. You get another round each time you re-roll this.

87 You are immune to fear from any kind of undead and are +1 to save vs any kind of spooky undead special power by any kind of ethereal dead. +2 more each time you re-roll this.

88-89 Cold does 2 points less damage to you for each time you roll this result.

90 On the first round of any combat (and only on the first round) you may gamble any number of your hit points on an attack. If you hit, you do that much damage; if you miss, you take that much damage (a miss indicates your foe was able to set up to receive your charge). You must be in the first rank of combatants (i.e. nobody gets to soften them up or test them before you pick how much you're gambling.) Each time you re-roll this you get +1 damage to the attack.

91-92 You can make your own weapons given a week and 10% of the usual cost of this merchandise. Each time you roll this (including the first time) you've had enough free time and luck to custom-craft one for your hand and fighting style, allowing you a +1 to hit and damage with that weapon.

93-94 Your scars, tattoos, and monstrous speech speak of exotic lands and distant adventure to the gullible folk of civilized lands. +2 to lie about where you've been or what you've seen to any of these so-called "sophisticates"; they'll believe anything. +2 more each time you re-roll this.

95 +2 to save vs any divine spell, +3 if you have personally slain a Cleric of that faith. +1 more each time you re-roll this.

96 On a successful hit you may distribute the damage rolled between any two targets within reach so long as they have an equal or lesser armor rating to the one you just hit. Every time you re-roll this you get one more target up to a maximum of 5.

97-98 You have a Stealth score of 2 in 6—add one each time you re-roll this result.

99-00 You have a Climb score of 2 in 6—add one each time you re-roll this result.

Witches
as player characters

REFEREES MAY WISH to make Witches available as player characters. Although mechanically similar to Magic-Users, Witches are conceptually more akin to hermit Clerics serving a host of unpopular gods (or demons); their power comes from rites performed and forces propitiated, not necessarily from studying texts. The male equivalent of the Witch is the Warlock, which is a slightly less evocative concept and—in this author's opinion—less fun.

In an ongoing campaign, I suggest making this option "unlock" as soon as a PC is slain by a witch. In the Lamentations of the Flame Princess system, at first level, the Witch has the following stats:

HP: 1d6
TO HIT: +1
SPELLS: 1 first level spell.
Language of Scales: All Witches can read the skins of serpents.

EACH TIME YOU level up roll once on the d100 Random Witch Traits chart and once on the d100 Witch Magical Abilities chart (pg 110).

Level	Experience	HP	Paralyze	Poison	Breath	Device	Magic	1	2	3	4	5	6	7	8	9
					Saving throws			Maximum spells per level								
1	0	1d6	13	13	16	13	14	1								
2	2,250	+1d4	13	13	16	13	14	2								
3	4,500	+1d4	13	13	16	13	14	2	1							
4	9,000	+1d4	13	13	16	13	14	2	2							
5	18,000	+1d4	13	13	16	13	14	3	2	1						
6	36,000	+1d4	11	11	14	11	12	3	2	2						
7	72,000	+1d4	11	11	14	11	12	3	3	2	1					
8	144,000	+1d4	11	11	14	11	12	4	3	2	2					
9	288,000	+1d4	11	11	14	11	12	4	3	3	2	1				
10	432,000	+1*	11	11	14	11	12	4	4	3	2	2				
11	576,000	+1*	9	9	12	9	8	5	4	3	3	2	1			
12	720,000	+1*	9	9	12	9	8	5	4	4	3	2	2			
13	864,000	+1*	9	9	12	9	8	5	5	4	3	3	2	1		
14	1,008,000	+1*	9	9	12	9	8	6	5	4	4	3	2	2		
15	1,152,000	+1*	9	9	12	9	8	6	5	5	4	3	3	2	1	
16	1,296,000	+1*	6	7	8	5	6	6	6	5	4	4	3	2	2	
17	1,440,000	+1*	6	7	8	5	6	7	6	5	5	4	3	3	2	1
18	1,584,000	+1*	6	7	8	5	6	7	6	6	5	4	4	3	2	2
19	1,728,000	+1*	5	6	7	4	4	7	7	6	5	5	4	3	3	2
20	+144,000/lvl	+1*/lvl	5	6	7	4	4	8	7	6	6	5	4	4	3	2

*Constitution modifiers no longer apply

D100 Random Witch Traits

Reroll redundant results.

1. By concentrating, you can cause any sleeping creature you have observed before to open its eyes and look around for 3 rounds, during which you can see through its eyes.
2. On a failed save of any kind, you begin to have an urge to steal an animal—it lasts 24 hours.
3. During storms, you can feel lightning as if it were a whip on your back.
4. Can curse a pregnant creature that has wronged you to have a deformed birth by sticking your tongue out at it.
5. You always know how many children and sexual partners any woman has had, so long as you can smell her.
6. Sour milk with a glance.
7. One finger has a small ring of flame.
8. Left hand has an unbreakable grip.
9. Dancing on a grave allows you to trigger illness in any single living family member of the deceased that has wronged you.
10. Sometimes your arms bend back and other parts of your body contort allowing you to squeeze through child-sized spaces.
11. Given 24 hours, you can use your blood and saliva and other secretions to make a potent hallucinogen that lasts 15 minutes.
12. You can make any man cry by speaking the name of what he fears.
13. You can heal scars caused by loved ones.
14. Cats, birds or wolves spy for you, delivering one observation per night.
15. Once per day, birds will steal small items for you, leaving items you give them of equal size.
16. Uncanny ability to quickly learn foreign languages, written or spoken, lip read, sign languages, codes—3 in 6 chance.
17. Can only bathe in fresh snowmelt.
18. Covetous desire for beautiful clothes and finery.
19. Can mimic any sound heard that day once.
20. Sucking on boiled white cat bones will turn you invisible.
21. You can identify potions on sight.
22. One of your five senses is extraordinary.
23. Unable to look any creature in the eye except your own reflection, which you find intoxicating beyond all measure.
24. Functional extra eye in a place of your choice.
25. The fingers of one hand can smell like any substance you desire, the touch of this hand leaves a trace that smells that way for twenty-four hours afterward.
25. Hair turns white and strong as steel.
26. Third nipple, secretes an ingestive poison that does d6 damage and causes the victim to vomit each round until a save is made.
27. Trolls fear you.
28. Grow horns like a goat or ram.
29. Forked tongue.
28. Flowering plants take d8 damage within 5' of you.
29. You may communicate with any family member by placing a message written in any enemy's blood into a special box the size of a ring box.
30. Corrosive saliva: d4 damage.
31. One eye is removable and continues to function if removed.
32. Skin becomes scaly. +1 armor rating.
33. Frog-like fly-catching tongue.
34. Fingernails hard as claws. D4 damage.
35. A demon (as *Summoning* spell) appears as you pray, it will share your bed and serve you one day a month.
36. Warts. Sorry.
37. Blemish in the shape of a murdered child.
38. Extra mouth where your eye should be.
39. No mouth. Cannot speak.
40. You have a scar that can speak and it speaks the true names of all you meet.
41. Colors in any room shift toward red along the spectrum—yellow becomes orange, green becomes yellow, blue becomes green, etc.
42. Mirrors break when you look at them.
43. Children in your presence ask impertinent questions of all adults nearby.
44. Domesticated animals panic in your presence.
45. You may prepare a small wax doll—as you are wounded, so, too, will it be (intentional wounds do not count). At the end of one month, you may melt the doll down into a paste which can be spread on one blade one time. The blade will inflict damage equal to the damage you took during the month on its first successful strike.
46. Books change to unknown languages in your hands.

47 When your tears reach the ground they begin to creep across the earth toward the nearest murderer.

48 You can spin small webs with your fingers, at the rate of an ordinary spider.

49 You cannot die by fire (though it can hurt you).

50 If you sleep in a garden for ten minutes it will swallow you into the earth and keep you there, unharmed and undetectable, as long as you wish.

51 You have no wrists. Hands function normally suspended a few inches above the end of your forearm.

52 You have the shadow of an animal. Somewhere an animal has yours.

53 You can appear up to 50 years older once per day.

54 You can appear up to 50 years younger once per day.

55 One of your little fingers is shaped like a scorpion tail and can deliver poison like one. Paralysis each round until save is made.

56 You can eat wood and metabolize it into rats.

57 You can heal others' wounds by taking them on yourself—it's all or nothing though, you can't take just part of someone's hp damage.

58 You know a song that puts animals to sleep, requires 30 unmolested seconds of singing.

59 If you and another woman stab each other with knives and leave them in, you can join your lives together, splitting all damage from any source evenly until the knives are removed.

60 Anyone having sexual intercourse with you will transform into a toad.

61 Your soul is stored in any object smaller than you that you desire. No clerical magic may affect you—but no magical healing either—unless it is cast on the soul as well.

62 Mice live in your pack or equipment, they make a lot of noise when they sense danger. They are not obedient.

63 Lanterns and torches dim in your presence (within 50' of you), reducing their radius by half.

64 Freshwater touching you becomes salt water. You cannot drink ordinary water.

65 Sounds echo around you confusingly. Nothing within 50' of you is easy to precisely locate by sound alone.

66 Spiders follow you.

67 Bats eat your fallen foes.

68 Wedding bands within 50' of you begin to constrict. Victims must Con check successfully each round or lose a finger for d3 points of damage.

69 You may not enter a properly-kept house through the door.

70 Precious gems and minerals appear to be worthless rock within 50' of you.

71 If someone sleeps in their bed after you have made it, their gender will change.

72 Fires double in intensity within 50' of you.

73 You can desecrate a church merely by entering it, and if you fornicate in one it will begin to decay at a rate of 10'/day.

74 You can steal the face from an unconscious creature for 5 minutes.

75 You have a 3 in 6 chance of speaking the language of any kind of animal (mockingbird, shrew, etc.) write down the ones you do and don't know.

76 While you sleep you are a black goat.

77 You may speak to the dead for ten minutes after midnight.

78 Sharp teeth. Bite for d4 damage.

79 Inanimate corpses fall to pieces at your touch.

80 Anything you sew or knit using cloth from the graves of the dead grants the wearer an extra save vs cold, but gives them nightmares.

81 Clerics and other devout folk cannot look directly at you.

82 Your kiss renders the kissed body part numb for 24 hours.

83 Virgins cannot harm you.

84 Immune to poison if you have eaten that day.

85 Any intelligent creature attracted to human women whose Wis is half of yours or less that sees you in moonlight must save vs Magic or be Charmed.

86 You cannot sleep except on the bare earth.

87 Holy symbols begin to rust and corrode in your presence.

88 Once a month an animal will ask a favor of you that will take approximately one day to complete and will be worth experience. You must obey or lose hp per day thereafter.

89 Gain a familiar: snakkur.

90 Gain a familiar: snake.

91 Gain a familiar: troll-cat.

92 Gain a familiar: cat.

93 Gain a familiar: toad.

94 Gain a familiar: newt.

95 Gain a familiar: rat.

96 Gain a familiar: dog.

97 Gain a familiar: ferret/marmot.

98 Gain a familiar: bat.

99 Gain a familiar: hare.

00 Gain a familiar: pig.

d100 Witch Magical Abilities

1-40 Choose a spell from the Witch or Magic-User list that is within your Maximum spells per level.

41-68 Choose a spell from the Witch or Cleric list that is within your Maximum spells per level.

69 I sense a great disturbance etc. etc. You have a form of postcognition that allows you to detect the presence of cast spells, eldritch creatures and the like (not omnipresent magic or currently magical things going on like Detect Magic could) in a given 30' x 30' area within the last day. You will know whether it was a spell or creature or effect or what. Re-rolling this allows you to know the nature of it broadly (enchantment, demon, etc.). Re-rolling this a third time tells you exactly what it is. Re-rolling it a fourth time allows you to function as a walking "Detect Magic" spell. After that re-roll.

70 Further advancement will require you to placate obscure gods. You have to adopt a taboo like:

† Cannot eat vegetables or meat.

† Cannot wash yourself.

† Cannot cut your hair.

† Cannot wear a certain color.

or whatever. Each time you re-roll this you need to take up another one.

71 Witch Lie. You can tell one lie per day (one sentence long) and be automatically believed by anyone at least half your level (round up). Re-rolling this means you can tell two lies, then three, etc.

72 After long eons of patient and lonely research you've found it—that thing you wanted? The Star Swallower? The dragon egg? The mountain fortress? It's there. 4 sessions worth of adventure away or less. Tell your Referee, who then must place it.

You must have a fair shot at it, like any other treasure, but there's no guarantee you will get it. If you don't get it by the fourth session you can keep trying or let it go and roll again on this table. However, if you choose to roll again and then you do get the thing somehow anyway, you lose whatever gimmick you rolled. Referee think up some clever reason why.

73-74 You may choose one of your spells that works at a touch, without any verbal component.

75-76 You have glimpsed primal vistas both horrific and majestic in your meditations. The flesh world does not concern you. Immune to fear. If you re-roll this, your companions gain a +2 vs fear if they can see you, then +4, etc.

77 By making a successful saving throw vs Magic you may turn any spell cast on anyone in line of sight back on the original caster. It is done immediately and you lose your next turn. You can do this once per day. Each time you re-roll this result you get +1 to the save.

78 +2 to save vs Magic. +1 more every time you roll this.

79-80 You may ask and receive an honest answer from an inanimate object once per day, plus one more every time you re-roll this. Inanimate objects aren't smart, but they know what has gone on around them.

81 Take a spell you already possess and bind it into an object. You may now use the spell twice per day and it functions as if you were a level higher. However: the spell is now bound to that object, not you. Whoever has the object can use it. Non-witches and lower-level witches use it as if it were cast by a witch one level lower than you.

82 Receive a random Witch or Magic-User spell one level higher than you are ordinarily able to cast.

83 One of your existing spells (pick one) is also attached to a form of the Contingency spell. A second "copy" of the spell is set to activate as soon as a trigger event of the caster's choice occurs. The caster may only cast and set a new contingency once a week. In essence, contingency means that rather than having 7 copies of a spell per week at will, the caster now has 8, but the 8th one is only activated by the specific condition. Re-rolling this result allows for another contingency to be set with a different spell.

84 Poorly grasped spell. You may select any spell of a level you are not normally allowed to cast, only it has a 50% chance of backfiring. Re-rolling this result improves the caster's odds by 1%. Only spells which would be dangerous or harmful if they backfired may be chosen.

85 Receive 2 random Witch or Cleric spells of any level you are able to cast.

86 Roll under Int +1 on a d20 to identify obscure pieces of lore and magic items. This ability goes far beyond what an ordinary Magic-User would know. Add +1 for each time you re-roll this until you get to 19.

87 You get one 8th lvl spell of your choice as a ritual (9th lvl if you are able to cast 8th lvl spells). This means either (your choice):

    † it takes 24 minus your Int score hours to cast it and you have to stay in the same place (30' x 30' square) doing nothing else the whole time, or...

    † you have to do some elaborate ritual thing that takes only an hour as described by the Referee for this effect.

Either way the target/area of effect must be right there unless you have a separate scrying spell or the like and the spell must be used immediately. You may cast your ritual spell once per month. Rolling this again gets you another one available.

88 +1 to hit every time you roll this.

89 You have a mutation that goes beyond mere deformity: an eye that floats an inch outside of its socket, a third arm, etc. You can roll a random mutation if you like or pick something.

90 You may write a magical contract. Anyone freely agreeing to such contract and signing it will take d6 damage per your level if they break it. The damage goes up by one die every time you re-roll this.

91 You may cast *Summon* once per month in addition to your normal complement of spells.

92 On a successful Wis check you can read both the aspect and aura of anyone at least 2 HD lower than your level. You know if they're lying, if they are under magical influence, and if they are what they seem. Re-rolling this adds one to the check.

93 On a successful save against Magic you not only successfully resist a spell, you may "catch" it and release it any time in the next 8 hours—effectively casting that spell as if it were your own. You may not cast any other spells until you release the stored spell. This only works on spells that affect only you or an area only you and/or your familiar occupy (like if *Rock to Mud* was cast and you were the only one in the room, you could absorb that). If you re-roll this result, you may use it on spells targeting you and one other person, if you re-roll it again then it goes for you and 2 other targets, etc. etc.

94 You know a magical recipe: you may cook a meal that transmits the effect of any spell you are able to cast. It takes a number of hours equal to the level of the spell to prepare, goes bad after 24 hours and feeds a number of creatures equal to your level.

95 You can turn into one other chosen shape at will. It can be another humanoid shape, like another person—or it can be an ordinary animal somewhere between your size and cat size. You have to decide what the thing is: its stats are exactly the same as yours and it has no special movement or sensory powers. I mean, if it's smaller than you it can move through smaller doors but otherwise whatever. Each time you re-roll this you get one other shape you can assume.

96 You have one spell of any level you are able to cast which is totally random each morning. Roll to see what it is. Re-rolling this result means you get another one plus one extra random spell each morning. And if you re-roll it again you get another plus two extra, etc.

97 You hover an inch above the ground at all times because magic. If the ground falls out from under you, you still fall, you just land an inch above where you normally would. -d6 to all falling damage. -d6 more each time you re-roll this result.

98 Your unnatural metabolism no longer handles what humans call "food". You eat something else—pick—it must be something that might be present in a forest but not in a bare prison cell. Likewise, your blood, tears, sweat, saliva, etc. no longer "taste" human and there is a 1 in 6 chance carnivores will ignore you. This chance goes up by one each time you reroll this result.

99-00 If you sleep, you will receive a minor prophecy in a dream. It will communicate some true or likely thing about the outcome of whatever's on your mind as you sleep.

Witch Spells of the Devoured Land

THESE SPELLS are available to Witches according to the rules above and may be learned by Magic-Users if the Referee so approves. When inscribed on scrolls, they made be read by any kind of character of any level and are cast at the reader's level.

Witch Spells by Level

D100 numbers included to generate a random Witch Scroll

Level	d100	Spell
1	1–6	Caress into Oblivion
	7–12	Cold Winds of Funeral Dust
	13–17	Internal Stoats
2	18–22	Cruel Curse
	23–27	Drown in Ashes
	28–32	Frozen by Icewinds
	33–37	Snowblind
3	38–41	Drunk's Reversal
	42–43	Blizzard Beasts
	44–47	Chain of Skin
	48–51	Paranoia
	52–56	Reanimate Dead Wood
	57–61	Sweet Leaf
	62–66	Web of Thorns
4	67–71	Fruits of Stupidity
	72–76	Spontaneous Amputation
5	77–80	Domain of Decay
	81–84	Nightmare Frenzy
	85–88	Wheels of Confusion
6	89–91	Hand of Doom
	92–94	Poison Eye
7	95–96	Feast of Claws
	97–98	Spell Epidemic
8	99	Arctic Swarm
9	00	Frostdemonstorm

Arctic Swarm

Level: 8
Duration: See below
Range: 0
Area of Effect: 20 mile radius
Save: No

TINY, LOCUST-LIKE INSECTS made of frost appear across the landscape, consuming every edible foodstuff, plant and defenseless game animal in the area of effect—even iron rations. Only magic can protect a foodstuff. The creatures finish their work and dissolve in an hour. Ordinary fishing, hunting, etc. here is impossible for at least a month—parties will have to eat things that fight back.

Blizzard Beasts

Level: 3
Duration: 1rnd/caster lvl
Range: 0
Area of Effect: 10' x caster lvl radius
Save: No

EVERY ENEMY CREATURE in the (necessarily snow-covered) area of effect is confronted with a shambling and hostile version of themselves made of ice and snow. The doppelganger has the same abilities but half the hit points and is effectively unarmored. The creatures begin to attack on the round the spell is cast.

Caress into Oblivion

Level: 1
Duration: 1 round per level
Range: Touch
Area of Effect: Area defined by 3 linear inches of cutting per level
Save: No

CASTER TRACES A FLAT shape with their hand in the air or on a surface up to 3 linear inches per level. This creates a hole in space in that shape, as if the fabric of reality had been cut with scissors. Anything that goes through it will never come back.

Chain of Skin

Level: 3
Duration: 3 rounds per level
Range: Touch
Area of Effect: See below
Save: No

WIZARD TOUCHES A TARGET skin-to-skin. That target becomes glued to the wizard. Any new creature touching the target becomes inextricably glued to the target and anyone touching that new creature becomes glued to them on and on.

Cold Winds of Funeral Dust

Level: 1
Duration: Instantaneous
Range: 0
Area of Effect: 40' cone
Save: vs Breath Weapon to dodge

WHEN THIS SPELL IS UTTERED, a fresh human or humanoid corpse (dead within the hour) freezes and then disintegrates into dust—these then blow in a strong wind away from the caster. Whoever the windborne dust touches must save vs Breath Weapon or take damage equal to (caster level) x (caster level).

Cruel Curse

Level: 2
Duration: 1 day per level + special
Range: 100'
Area of effect: 1 creature per level
Save: vs Magic to negate

TO TRIGGER THE CURSE, the caster must observe the target (any creature with fewer HD than the caster) perform the same action for at least two consecutive rounds. The caster may then invoke one of two effects:

a) The target creature must continuously do one thing chosen by the caster that it was doing in the last two turns,

or...

b) the target can never do some chosen thing it was doing in the last two turns.

The repeated/forbidden action cannot be anything the creature normally always does (breathe, touch the ground, etc.). The effect of the curse can be something that will probably kill the creature in its current circumstance but it cannot be something that would inevitably kill it regardless of circumstance. For example: the curse could not compel a creature to stop breathing but it could compel a creature to continue walking in a straight line even if that line (in that particular situation) would lead it off a cliff.

No two *Cruel Curses* may be identical (which is why curses tend to be weirdly specific).

If the caster has at least 7 HD more than the target, the curse is permanent until *Remove Curse* or a specific task (see **Breaking Curses** for examples) is performed. If the caster has at least 10 HD more than the victim, *Remove Curse* will not work, and only a task can free the victim.

Domain of Decay

Level: 5
Duration: Permanent
Range: 0
Area of Effect: 1' per caster level radius, centered on caster
Save: No

ALL NON-MAGICAL, NONLIVING things in the area of effect age until they are useless and ruined—food, armor, walls, clothes etc.

Drown in Ashes

Level: 2
Duration: Permanent
Range: 0
Area of Effect: (caster level x 10') radius
Save: vs Breath Weapon

A WAVE OF ASH, 6" deep per caster level fills the area of effect. Anything living with its head below the surface must save vs Breath Weapon or be buried, taking d4 choking damage per round until they do save.

Drunk's Reversal

Level: 3
Duration: Permanent
Range: LOS
Area of Effect: 2 targets
Save: See below

TWO TARGETS IN LINE of sight (typically one drunk and one not) swap levels of inebriation. Basically. If the targets are different sizes it's a little more complicated: if one party is originally drunk and small and the other is sober and large, the larger party will have a bonus to save vs Poison in proportion to the size disparity. If the sober party is small, there is no save.

Feast of Claws

Level: 7
Duration: See below
Range: 30'
Area of Effect: 100 mile radius around target
Save: No

ALL PREDATORY ANIMALS in the area of effect stop what they are doing and move as swiftly as they can to attack a chosen target until it is destroyed or the caster is. The spell may target an object rather than a creature, in which case the animals come to where the object is and attack anyone present.

To determine what animals arrive, essentially roll a random encounter check for the area every round—any ordinary predator indicated has arrived. If the Referee has no random encounter table, roll a d20 each round, on a result of 1-6 a predator appropriate to the area of the indicated number of HD has come into view, if the roll is greater than that, no creature has arrived that round.

FrostDemonstorm

Level: 9
Duration: Until concentration ends or Hell is empty
Range: 10'
Area of Effect: -
Save: No

TWO FROST DEMONS under the caster's control appear from the snow every round that the caster does nothing else but concentrate. Frost demons are in most ways like drowning demons (see **Drowning Demons**) except they try to suffocate you in snow instead of drown you. They melt away at the next sunrise.

Frozen by Icewinds

Level: 2
Duration: See below
Range: 10'
Area of Effect: 50' cone
Save: vs Paralysis to negate

A CHILL WIND blows, everyone who fails is frozen in a sheath of ice until they make a Str check or someone outside does (or melts the ice). The maximum HD of creatures that can be affected is equal to the caster's level.

Fruits of Stupidity

Level: 4
Duration: Permanent
Range: 0
Area of Effect: An apple-sized meal
Save: No

THE CASTER TOUCHES one foodstuff of any kind and offers it to any intelligent creature—it cannot be forced on the target and the target can be in no way deceived as to the nature of the caster's identity. If the creature takes a bite, chews and swallows, the caster is in complete control of the eater forever.

Hand of Doom

Level: 6
Duration: 4 rounds
Range: -
Area of Effect: Caster
Save: No

ONE OF THE CASTER'S HANDS transforms—becoming blackened, seething—and capable of disintegrating 6" cube of whatever it touches, including living things, magic items, whatever. The actual touching can start the next round.

Internal Stoats

Level: 1
Duration: Instantaneous
Range: 10'
Area of Effect: 20' x 20' x 20' cube
Save: No

STOATS BEGIN CLAWING their way out from inside the body of everyone within the area of effect, emerging from their mouths and from holes of their own creation. The stoats will do 3 points of damage per caster level, spread evenly between all creatures in the area of effect.

Nightmare Frenzy

Level: 5
Duration: 3 rounds
Range: 5'
Area of Effect: 20' x 20' area
Save: Partially negates

TELL THE PARTY that demons spring from the ground. They don't, though. Actually, everyone in the area of effect is afflicted by terrifying visions of everyone else in the area of effect. There is no save against the visions—however the targets do get a save vs Magic to avoid attacking each other, thinking they're demons. Which they'll do otherwise.

Paranoia

Level: 3
Duration: 1 hr per level
Range: Whispering distance
Area of Effect: See below
Save: No

WIZARD WHISPERS A WARNING into a target's ear. Target then must whisper the same warning into the ear of everyone it meets (Targets must do this for 2 hours, and new targets are enchanted until 1/hr per caster's level has passed). It may or may not believe the warning, but cannot tell anyone that until the spell ends.

Poison Eye

Level: 6
Duration: Permanent
Range: 40'
Area of Effect: One eye
Save: No

ONE OF THE TARGET'S EYES becomes poisonous to the rest of its body, inflicting d8hp per round. The effect stops if the eye is removed, but doing this causes d20hp and, of course, they just lost an eye.

Reanimate Dead Wood

Level: 3
Duration: see below
Range: 20'
Area of Effect: caster level radius in feet
Save: No

EVERY WOODEN OBJECT or part of an object in the radius comes alive (sword hilts, bootheels, etc.) sprouts rootlike tentacles and begins to attack the caster's foes. Each object has the stats of a rat (aside from the diseases) or, if it's larger, the stats of an animal of equivalent size. An end-table would likely attack as a dog, for instance. The attacks subside when the objects' hp are depleted but all the objects are useless afterward until reworked.

Snowblind

Level: 2
Duration: d4 rounds
Range: 0
Area of Effect: Line of sight
Save: vs Magic to negate

EVERYONE VISIBLE must save or be blinded. Only works in snow. A total HD of creatures equal to the caster's level may be affected.

Spell Epidemic

Level: 7
Duration: Variable
Range: 0
Area of effect: Variable
Save: vs Magic to negate

A HOSTILE SPELL (and only a hostile spell) which targets the witch alone is intensified so that it also affects a number of targets of the witch's choice equal to the witch's level. The spell activates as soon as the hostile spell takes effect, and means the witch loses their next turn.

Spontaneous Amputation

Level: 4
Duration: Permanent
Range: 60'
Area of Effect: 1 creature
Save: vs Magic to negate
TARGET'S ARM falls off.

Sweet Leaf

Level: 3
Duration: Permanent
Range: 30'
Area of Effect: One creature
Save: vs Poison to negate
TARGET BECOMES ADDICTED to the last vegetable substance he or she willingly ingested by any means. The target must have it every day in a quantity just large enough to be unhealthy. If it is unavailable, the target will begin to experience withdrawal: -1 to everything, then -2 the next day, then -3, etc. until the substance is acquired. Remove Curse or the like will fix it.

Web of Thorns

Level: 3
Duration: 5 rounds
Range: 50'
Area of Effect: 30' x 30' area
Save: vs Breath Weapon to jump out of the way
THORNED PLANTS SPRING UP and entrap everyone—like Web only it inflicts d6hp per round you're stuck in it.

Wheels of Confusion

Level: 5
Duration: See below
Range: 10' per level
Area of Effect: 1 creature
Save: No
TARGET ACTS AS if under a *Confusion* spell for 4 rounds and then for 4 rounds again each hour thereafter until *Remove Curse* or the like is cast. The target likely will likely mistake this for a regular *Confusion* spell at first.

New Substances

Ektesvarsk

EKTESVARSK IS A METAL found only in the Devoured Land. It is incredibly resilient and light-absorbent—both of which properties are due either to its unusual carbon-nanotube structure or to having been made from the shadows of fallen gods. Items forged of Ektesvarsk are so black as to seem utterly featureless save upon the closest inspection. An ektesvarsk blade does +1 damage, is immune to magic, and looks like a hole in the sky.

It is occasionally mistaken for a more common material called Falsksvarsk, which is much weaker, and reflects whatever is nearby, but poorly.

Forgetting Dust

ON A FAILED SAVE you forget the last day—keep rolling until you succeed or fail four times. Two failed saves means you forget the last month. Three and you forget the last year. Four, you forget who you are.

Witherbound Powder

WEAPONIZED VERSION of the lichen-based hallucinogen used by The Thirteen. Save vs Poison each round or suffer random hallucination (d20):

1. A flash flood is coming and the nearest creature of equal or larger size is a tree—start climbing.
2. Largest weapon in line of sight is your long-lost lover—embrace them.
3. Everything writhes as if you're standing on an immense belly, grab and hold nearest object.
4. You no longer recognize your tongue and think there is a fat wet maggot in your mouth.
5. Your friends are on fire—put them out!
6. You're a whale.
7. You have a massive wound in your chest you must tend to—strip away clothes and armor to get to it.
8. They're all after you—flee friend and foe alike.
9. The enemy is reading your surface thoughts and will burrow in further soon—knock yourself unconscious so you can't betray yourself.
10. You're a scarecrow in a high wind.
11. You are a fang in the mouth of the great serpent that girds the world.
12. You are an echo—repeat what you hear and do nothing else.
13. You are the lord of this world—why are your children unruly? Demand they behave but do not sully yourself by quarreling with them.
14. You are beneath a black ocean—climb as high as you can so you can breathe again.
15. A frost giant approaches—everyone must be quiet!
16. Hah! You're invisible!
17. You stare down the dividing branches into the spiral of time, through unknown aeons into the eyes of your god. It speaks to you.
18. You are a cobweb.
19. You are a child pretending to be an adventurer, wearing clothes too big for you. Why don't they understand?
20. Finally the treasure—everything you see is made of gold. Put it in a sack.

Survival Skills in the Devoured Land

BUSHCRAFT IS AN ESPECIALLY useful skill in the uninviting environs surrounding Mount Hellebor and the Slith. Some specific uses of survival skills are noted below:

Herb Lore

GENERALLY PERMA-NENT Amazon camps have herbs neces-sary to provide some degree of medical care to the injured. Friendly visitors can expect to regain 2 hit points per day if tended.

All NPC Amazon witches and any other NPC Amazon with an Intelligence of at least 14 are initiated into the arts of mid-wifery and embryoc-tony. NPC witches and NPC Amazons with an Intelligence over 16 have a degree of skill in pathology.

Any unusual operation will require tinctures prepared from herbs. If the NPCs Amazons make a successful Bushcraft check at minus 1 the neces-sary materials are immediately on hand. If they are not, they will need to be gathered—herbs neces-sary for managing pain, infection inducing labor can be gathered in any area adjoining the river on a successful Bushcraft check, but abortifiacients can only be found reliably in quantity in area F3—on the Eastern slope of Mount Hellebor.

Any character with at least 2 in Bushcraft can be taught to identify the appropriate herbs on sight.

Hunting

WORMS OR OTHER CATASTROPHES can easily beset a party's supply of provisions in the Devoured Land. Many creatures will target a party's food supply and then flee. Acquiring new food is neither easy nor trivial.

Survival hunting requires a successful Bushcraft roll and takes half an hour. On a failed roll, roll an encounter check instead (see Random Encounters pg 138). After the encounter is resolved, the hunter may roll another Bushcraft check.

Negotiating With Animals

ANIMALS IN THE DEVOURED Land are all intelligent, even if they do not share a language with a given human. A successful Bushcraft roll will allow a character to recognize this immediately, and subsequent ones will allow an adventurer to recall simple facts about what animals in the mundane world usually want ("wolves like meat") but will not allow them access to Devoured-Land-specific information ("these wolves will not rest until they've killed at least one of us"). Beasts can be negotiated with via nonver-bal communication like any other character—they recognize symbols, gestures, etc.

How to Make a Wilderness Sandbox

How to Make a Wilderness Sandbox

THE DEVOURED LAND MAP PROVIDED here can be used as part of a larger "sandbox"-style game—a campaign directed by players deciding what to do and where to go as they adventure across a map pre-seeded with possible targets and adventure hooks.

In a sandbox, the players should start with just enough information that they can choose from among a few options that seem interesting or profitable or both. The Referee should possess more information than the players about what's going on in the landscape, but isn't expected to have complete detailed descriptions of everything that's going on. Once your group starts moving, you'll have to improvise the details you haven't already nailed down.

A few things to remember:

† The map here has been cut into rectangles, so that it's easier to read what's in each area, however the traditional way to make a sandbox map is with tessellated hexagons (a "hexmap"). This is convenient—the distance from the center of any given hexagon to any adjacent hexagon is equal.

† A common size for hexagons is 6 miles across because it's three miles to the horizon over flat ground—so if a party is in the middle of a hex, they can theoretically see some landmarks in adjoining hexes.

† The players will be either traveling overland from point to point (moving at traveling speed) and just running into stuff incidentally or carefully searching through each hex individually (moving at "mapping" or "searching" speed— which is slower). Which on they're doing at any point depends on the kind of campaign goals they have (like this one is all about mapping, while these involve both traveling and searching). If, for example, you need to get to a castle to deliver a message you're traveling, if you're trying to conduct a survey and create a map of an area, you're searching.

† Searching characters are trying to find all the interesting things in an area. Traveling characters will only note the obvious stuff (mountains, huge rivers) or things that find them (angry cultists, desperate bandits, etc)

† The key to this kind of thing is meaningful choices and choices require information. There are two traditional ways hexcrawling players can get information: A. They start with a partial map, B. They look around.

† In either case, these two ways of encountering the landscape should be calculated as much as possible to present players with at least two options for how to go at all times. For traveling, the simplest choice is: Fast, dangerous route or slow, easier route. Of course the slow route is also dangerous because it gives more time to run into random encounters.

† If the players just look around (no map), they will see landmarks. Landmarks are extremely important. These are things PCs can see in different directions that indicate what kind of thing to expect in that direction--mountain? City? Monument? River? Without landmarks the players are just going "Hmm, east or west?" and that's totally arbitrary and boring because there's no information behind it.

† Players walk (or ride) and you keep track of time (figure out movement speeds per hour and per day for whatever method the PCs are using). When you get to a new area figure out what's obvious and (if your players are searching) what's hidden. Tell them about the obvious thing right off, "So you ride for an hour and then you see a massive rock shaped like an eagle".

† Random encounters are important—as are the way they interact with the landscape. Without them, the environment is static, not to mention far too safe. With random encounters, the landscape becomes more than just what you seeded into the map—if the party randomly meets a witch near the eagle-shaped rock, that rock could end up becoming the place where a portal into another dimension is first discovered. Let the encounter go where it needs to—don't treat it as a distraction from the "plot"—as soon as a creature is discovered, that is the plot.

† If there's an encounter, figure out whether the thing sees them or they see it first or whether they see each other simultaneously (just like a dungeon). Remember that since most hex products or maps you make are, of necessity, sketchy, you can and should embroider on what the PCs see. You do not have to stick to the description. "1047 River, Demon" can be turned into... "You see a bridge with an insect demon eating a giant pink ooze on it, there appears to be no other crossing here".

† Build up the setting around the players as they move. They meet a random Cleric? If you can figure out who this is a Cleric of and where the Cleric's going and what temple the Cleric is from you've just added lots of obstacles and resources for the players and added a layer to what's going on.

† At the end of a session, ask the players what they intend to do next session. You can prep more detail around their likely routes. The key to making a hexcrawl more than a bunch of random encounters is building relationships between locations on the map—a good hex map will have these seeded in to begin with, but there's always room for more.

† If your players are searching, remember there's lots of room in a hex for stuff no matter how small. All of Manhattan is only about two standard hexes long. Don't have any ideas? That's what all these random tables in the book are for.

† Many times, if they're just traveling, the PCs will come upon nothing special in a given hex, that's ok. It may not be that way the next time they pass through. The more familiar a party becomes with a landscape (Oh, that's the tree where Igor got sacrificed), the more they can use it and interact with it.

Random Tables

Adventure Elements

EVERY ADVENTURE should have something unique about it that matches the flavor of the Devoured Land—roll d100 below, pick from the list, or make up your own ideas and consider them in relation to what's already on the map. What connection might a stone immune to magic have to the murder of circling crows and the ruins of the old watchtower? Create a web of hidden connections to tie together what you already have and place the signs of trouble where the party is likely to run into them.

1   An axe's hilt emblazoned with a rampant beast.
2   A blonde prophet who suffers seizures.
3   Steel climbing claws.
4   Snow that falls in reverse.
5   A swordsman held for ransom.
6   A genealogical history dating back 5000 years.
7   Leeches gorged on the blood of a dead prince.
8   An obscene old man in woolen gloves.
9   A bride fleeing her wedding.
10 A stone immune to magic.
11 A copse where a bloodthirsty tribe are forbidden to shed blood.
12 Three scheming bastard daughters.
13 A criminal transformed into an animal.
14 A witch who enchants with a kiss.
15 A man with eyelids cut away, so he has no choice but to witness a contract.
16 A massive hourglass filled with snow.
17 A powerful amnesiac.
18 A fish that delivers a prophecy when caught.
19 A pit full of Amazon sacrifices.
20 A glove made from a stag's bladder—the hand that wears it cannot steal.
21 A spindle that spins clothes that can never be worn.
22 A skull overgrown with lichen.
23 Sausages made from men.
24 A misshaped lamb that cannot move and riddles like a sphinx.
25 A messenger killed by poison lingonberries.
26 A painful abscess filling with liquid silver.
27 A murder victim discovered as salmon buried to ferment are dug up.
28 Five overlapping vows of revenge.
29 The castle has fallen but a cursed gate remains.
30 A thing of literally aching beauty, its victims come willingly to stare and writhe on the ground.
31 A dusk that lasts a month.
32 A wolf that eats only grave dust.
33 Brandy flavored with giant spit.
34 A child's corpse disguised as a doll, with plum-pits for eyes.
35 A toad collecting cloudberries and holding them in its gullet.
36 A bag made from the stomach of a cutpurse.
37 A festival of secrets, where Amazons compete to reveal things least known.
38 A cheesemaking cave, fallen into disuse.
39 A sword that has split 1000 ribs.
40 A ceremony of hate-fucks and fire-eating .
41 Small animals crawling toward men hanging in vast webs and extending webs of their own entrails.
42 A home carved into the tooth of a giant.
43 A red mead that provokes mirthless laughter.
44 Lepers left to die on the ice.
45 A demon living in a cracked furnace.
46 A regenerating shield of trollskull.
47 A witch stitching together arms, severed at the shoulder, like spokes around a hub.
48 A giant that owes a favor to a raven.
49 A mirror that shows how you will look tomorrow.
50 A waterfall above rocks, used for executions. The dead lie pooled beneath the river.
51 The 'blood eagle'—foes slain by having their lungs torn out through their backs.

52 A poem of hate composed by a spurned lover.

53 A creek that glitters with old blood-rust from weapons washed upstream.

54 A hot spring where animals bathe.

55 A contest of boasting of beasts slain.

56 Runes that spell another message when turned sideways.

57 A misshaped bat, screeching wildly, unable to fly.

58 An ossuary box containing demon bones.

59 A long furrow in the snow formed by a horse dragging a dead rider.

60 A trollking resting in a pit full of spears.

61 A fat crow with a bellyfull of diamonds.

62 A witch who tells you where to find your lost love—whom she then pretends to be.

63 A memory suppressed until a magic word is spoken.

64 A powerful hostage from the cities, the ransom note sent tied round a wolf's neck.

65 A spell which destroys the house where it is cast.

66 A vain and contemptuous lord, brought low and fleeing in disguise.

67 Rabid deer run wild across the landscape like a disease.

68 A pair of evil shoes that cannot be destroyed nor lost.

69 A wicked duke scouring the land for a renowned witch.

70 A funeral barge pushed into the river, full of cursed gold.

71 A battle on a bridge.

72 An invisible house.

73 Box full of eggs of many species, being prepared to spawn a strange army.

74 A river choked with bloated dog carcasses.

75 A song that calls 5 giants.

76 A necklace of polished rat bones.

77 Women who have not seen a living man in 12 years.

78 A cave where a prisoner has been hanging from the ceiling for a month, fed and pricked by spiders.

79 A stalactite knife.

80 A hooded cloak that hides your tracks but makes you twice as hungry as normal.

81 Gauntlets of iron that, once wrapped around a witch, can never unclench.

82 An unbreakable chain of ektesvarsk.

83 A newt vomiting stones carved with the names of dead kings.

84 A cauldron that boils cold.

85 A boar sleeping on a pile of books in the Giftschrank of a Pearlholder church.

86 A bjära being tracked back to a witch's lair by a Cold Banner assassin.

87 A fisherman's boat returning to the shore full of straw men.

88 An earthquake reveals what appears to be a giant's hoard.

89 As lava spills toward a camp of Frostbitten Moons, the Maggot Sisters attack.

90 A snakkur drags mushrooms down a cliff face toward its mistress.

91 A pregnant duchess kneels at the feet of an Amazon midwife, offering a book full of secrets.

92 A fox creeps to the edge of a troll's pudding, about to make an offer to the creature boiling within.

93 A lantern made of jawbones, bringing silence and cold light.

94 An Amazon carries a wet sack of hearts.

95 A Frostbitten Moon milks a nest of adders and reads lessons from their skins.

96 Amazons unearth the rich, frozen grave of King Ovv's first murdered queen .

97 Rats rip into the belly of a bear, from which a wooden scroll case spills.

98 An iron spiked ball, dipped in herbs which make it seem tasty to stupid animals.

99 A wizard's apprentice being Charmed by an Ulvenbrigad witch and sent back to his party.

00 A white cat licks its paws, weeping blood.

Adventure Locations

To extend the Devoured Land—especially midgame—it's helpful to have a background of random features to build on top of. These procedures can be slightly modified for different kinds of places outside the mountainous boreal and subtundra landscapes described herein.

Landmarks

You can use this method to determine features that are visible at a distance—either when players look out on uncharted territory in game or while preparing a map. Start with a blank piece of graph paper, take *a handful of dice* (at least one of each kind will give a varied landscape, but you can pick and choose once you're used to the method) and drop it on the paper—

Discoverable Features

To randomly determine less obvious contents of an area, go from area to area on the graph paper and roll on the Random Encounter table (pg 138)once for each area—whatever you roll is there or makes its home there. If you only want landscape features and no creatures, roll d20, add 60 and then consult the Random Encounter table (generating a number from 61-80). Afterward add Adventure Hooks from the next table.

D4s indicate **mountains**, specifically:

1. Isolated peak (not part of a range).
2. High point of a range running east-west.
3. High point of a range running north-south.
4. Peak has another feature on top (roll any other die).

D6s indicate **ruins**:

1. Village.
2. Fortress/Castle.
3. Church.
4. Farm.
5. Watchtower or Bridge.
6. Inn.

D8s indicate **recent structures** and signs of habitation:

1. Hut or house.
2. Fortress.
3. Pearlholder church.
4. Watchtower.
5. Cave.
6. Bridge.
7. Graveyard.
8. Clearing.

D10S indicate **water**—All frozen from the Days of the Octopus and Squid (October) to the Days of the Threshold (April). For streams and rivers, orientation of number on die relative to the paper indicates the orientation of the flow.

1 River.
2 River with island.
3 River with waterfall.
4 Pond.
5 Fen or bog.
6 Creek.
7 Edge of a huge lake spanning multiple areas.
8 Lake.
9 Lake with an island in it.
10 Lake with waterfall.

D12S indicate **encampments and groups** large enough to be seen at a distance:

1 Frostbitten Moons.
2 Maggot Sisters.
3 Ulvenbrigad.
4 Other Amazons.
5 Hunters.
6 Wolves.
7 Deer.
8 Pearlholders.
9 Merchant caravan.
10 NPC party.
11 Mercenary troupe.
12 Wild horses.

D20S indicate **unusual sights**

1 Frost giant.
2 Volcano.
3 Massacre site.
4 Giant footprints (moving "up" relative to position of number on die).
5 Massive strange rock formation.
6 Wolf pack (actually werewolves).
7 Forest starts or stops here.
8 Field of broken ice.
9 Valley begins (oriented along direction of number on die).
10 Scientific/exploratory expedition.
11 Lone creature visible against the snow.
12 Circular copse of strange trees grown together.
13 Old stone wall unattached to any structure.
14 Large murder of crows circling something unseen.
15 Clearly visible tracks.
16 Fire.
17 Ship frozen in the ice.
18 Occult circle carved into lake ice.
19 Cliffs (land rises from party's point of view).
20 Cliffs (land drops off from party's point of view).

Amazon Divination Games

AMAZONS PRACTICE a form of adversarial divination using chess pieces carved from stag bone. Pawns are each named for a phase of the moon, the knight is replaced with the huntress, the bishop by the witch and the king by the demon.

Each player nominates an foe in the world to be represented by their opponent's demon—the primary purpose of the game is to determine the time and manner of death of that foe. Only the winner receives a divination, and its content is determined by the disposition of the pieces at the end of the game.

The important factor is the pieces (or pieces) that mate the defeated demon at the end of the game.

Discover the winner by whoever rolls better on an Int test, then see how the game ended by rolling below:

Method of Death (D8)

1 Closest enemy piece is a Queen. The foe will die by the winner's hand.
2 Closest enemy piece is a Tower. The foe will die of illness.
3 Closest enemy piece is a Huntress. The foe will die by a weapon.
4 Closest enemy piece is a Witch. The foe will die by sorcery.
5 Closest enemy piece is a Demon. The foe will die at the hand of the other player's foe.
6 Closest enemy piece is a Moon (Pawn). The foe will die by accident.
7–8 Roll two more times on this table.

Time of Death (D10)

The time is determined by the closest enemy moon at mate:

1 Foe will die during the New Moon.
2 Foe will die during the Waxing Crescent Moon.
3 Foe will die during the First Quarter Moon.
4 Foe will die during the Waxing Gibbous Moon.
5 Foe will die during the Full Moon.
6 Foe will die during the Waning Gibbous Moon.
7 Foe will die during the Third Quarter Moon.
8 Foe will die during the Waning Crescent Moon.
9 Roll d10 twice on this table, could be either.
10 No enemy Moon was on the board at the end, time of death is unclear (unless the result above was 6, in which case roll again).

ONCE A DIVINATION is set, the foe must roll twice and pick the lowest result when facing any situation that would directly lead to their death occurring in the foretold manner at the foretold time, and, likewise, their foes may roll any To Hit (or other similar) rolls on them twice and pick the highest if it would directly lead to the creature's death in the prescribed manner.

A foe's fate may only be discovered once via this method, though if a querent loses it may be sought again.

Further divinations can be derived from the disposition of the pieces and the occupied squares at the Referee's discretion using the Fortunes from *Vornheim: The Complete City Kit* if they have access to that estimable tome.

NEW MOON
WAXING CRESCENT
FIRST QUARTER
WAXING GIBBOUS
FULL
WANING GIBBOUS
THIRD QUARTER
WANING CRESCENT

TO WER
HUNTRESS
WITCH QUEEN
DEMON
WITCH HUNTRESS
TO WER

129

Amazon Tribes, New

FOR THE CREATION of new Amazon factions.

Identifying features:

1. They each have trained eagles or other animals.
2. Use a strange bluish pigment in war that grants them +2 to hit and -2 to Int for ten minutes.
3. Wear the skins of their forebears. Each Amazon must grow fat in their dotage so that the next generation may wear suits made from their skins and hide inside them. Nobody knows what they look like.
4. Piercings incorporating the teeth of foes slain.
5. Wear garish and mismatching patterns from many animals.
6. Wild hair, filled with small knives.
7. By bathing in honeys and unguents they are surrounded by halos of stinging and crawling things, harmless to them.
8. Their only clothes are the bones of those they've slain. So: new and untested Amazons have no clothes upon them because they never killed anyone and the old warmistresses have like bone armor so thick it's amazing they can move.
9. Their hierarchy has a color code. Different ranks dye their hair different colors.
10. Due to a genetic irregularity or ancient curse they are all twins.

Beliefs:

1. They don't believe in killing animals because they're innocent. Got no problem killing people though.
2. They believe the soul is contained in the right foot and will evince an unhealthy obsession with severing a foe's right foot, to the exclusion of all other hit locations. They wear heavy shoes.
3. They hate food and the eating of food. Publicly. In secret they all eat food (of course) and like it but in company they pretend they don't. It's weird.
4. They refuse to speak.
5. They believe they must remain hidden and undescribed, so they pluck out the eyes of any outsider they see.
6. They believe it is blasphemous to use anything that is not stolen. Their equipment, homes, mounts and mates are all stolen.
7. They believe that if they are defeated by anyone they'll be owned by them in the afterlife. Will always fight to the death—Morale 12.
8. They refuse to kill women but will attempt to capture and convert them.
9. They believe animals are wiser than men and swarm around any foe their warbeasts attack.
10. They believe that heaven is contained inside an anonymous rock hidden somewhere in the Devoured Land. They search for it.

Their totem:

1. Their totem is the locust. They gibber and swarm.
2. Their totem is the troll. They revel in ignorance.
3. Their totem is the jackal. They belong to treachery.
4. Their totem is the eel. They are patient, they are swift.
5. Their totem is the crow. They seek gold and the gleaming.
6. Their totem is the stag. They are proud and drink from rivers.
7. Their totem is the hog. They wallow and they wail.
8. Their totem is the spider. They are old and wise.
9. Their totem is a nine-pound hammer. They bash and bruise and boast.
10. Their totem is the scorpion. They live in solitude and strike in secret.
11. Their totem is the toad. Their lives are moist and dull.
12. Their totem is the centipede. They form a long lean line.
13. Their totem is a basking lizard. They dine on dogs and wine.
14. Their totem is a newt. They come from another time.
15. Their totem is a broken shackle. They were once a lower caste.
16. Their totem is the whiteblack leopard. They move in darkness.
17. Their totem is the dog. They harry and howl.
18. Their totem is the rat. They speak in whispers.
19. Their totem is the salamander. They will burn you.
20. Their totem is the bear. There are no children among them.

Their object of reverence:

1. A misshapen tree with unusual properties.
2. Goat butter. A mound of it.
3. Blood of many foes. In a great urn.
4. A sacred child or invalid.
5. The clothes once worn by a fallen leader.
6. A pitchfork.
7. The scales of a great white dragon.
8. The night, silence, quiet, stillness and stone.
9. A fat, four-footed weasel carved of lard, smothered in beets.
10. Severed fingers, kept in cloths.

Their leader:

1. An alchemist, who concocts powerful acids.
2. Belligerent, bony, bedecked with baubles. Surrounded by bats.
3. A crooked crone, a maker of candles.
4. A witch, served by a demon.
5. An enigmatic, laconic and largely sessile veteran, borne on a palanquin.
6. A fat flagellant.
7. A preening diva, fond of elaborate dress and wild spectacle.
8. A scholar of war with a great library.
9. An inquisitive and generous woman, eager for knowledge of the outside world's designs on her territory.
10. An ambitious child of 12.

Details on the tribe's leader:

1. She is hideous and clothed in shadow.
2. She has worms in her head.
3. She has a hump like a camel, filled with jewels.
4. She owes a PC a single favor.
5. She is subtle and sophisticated, and has secret dealings with women of the cities.
6. She is half troll.
7. She hopes to wage war against the moon.
8. She is a contortionist and able to twist her body into the shapes of the 32 symbols of The Divine.
9. She is drunk and silly but has a voice like an avalanche.
10. She is a schemer, secretly at the center of all events in the campaign.

Breaking Curses

1 Perform a service for each of 8 infamous heretics on 8 successive Saint's Days.
2 See the sea through the eyes of a hated foe.
3 Touch a wild horse with gloves of kidskin when the moon is waxing.
4 Sink a 3-masted ship sailed by a virgin.
5 Pile five toads on a pigpike and slay with it a mighty troll.
6 Kill the witch who cast the curse and the write her name in blood on the wall of every church for 30 miles.
7 Mold a statue of the moon goddess from the bones of wolves.
8 Blind a bishop.
9 Rescue a madman from a fornicator and send him into the ocean.
10 Make a powder from the bones of a lychewife felled by your own hand. Mix it with banewort and flywhile. Drink it.
11 Deliver justice to 20 random souls.
12 Murder a frost giant unaided while a noonday sun burns and the call of carrion birds echoes across the escarpments and pale plains of the colorless waste.
13 Rescue twelve innocents from death by hanging.
14 Drain the venom from the heads of 3 serpents into a summer fruit. Eat it.
15 Steal into the fastness of Cardinal Norngillian and replace five verses in the Codex of Nynglisten with blasphemous ones.
16 Collect the tongues of an astrologer.
17 Recover a rusted box from the bottom of Massacre Lake.
18 Scorn all offers of aid for ninety-nine days.
19 Contrive a confection of sugar, water, and hog gelatin, whip it to a spongy consistency, cast it and coat it in starches. Roast it over the flames of your most fearsome enemy. Consume it.
20 Consult a Tarot reader concerning the fortunes of 5 women, and then ensure these come to pass.

Confrontations

USE WHEN AN AREA contains two different groups of creatures: First creature(s) rolled are ___ second creature(s)

ROLL D20...

1 eating
2 killing
3 negotiating with a
4 selling something to
5 aiding a wounded
6 chasing
7 babbling about
8 hunting with the aid of
9 travelling with
10 seducing
11 eating several
12 killing several
13 negotiating with several
14 selling something to several
15 aiding wounded _____(s)
16 looking for several
17 babbling about several
18 hunting with the aid of several
19 travelling with several
20 seducing several

Deformations of the Misshaping Pool

ROLL ONCE FOR EACH round a creature or part of one is immersed in a Misshaping Pool.

Mutation (d20)

1 Tentacles.
2 Hair/feathers disappear(s).
3 Rotted appearance, skin hanging.
4 Elongated/enlarged body part (roll right)
5 Bloated body or body part (roll right).
6 A body part (roll right) duplicates.
7 Two body parts (roll right) transpose.
8 Covered in spines.
9 A body part (roll right) amputates.
10 Twisting horn.
11 Tusks.
12 A body part (roll right) shrinks.
13 Terrible useless wings.
14 Hole through chest.
15 Asymmetrical body.
16 Intestines hanging out.
17 Translucent skin.
18 Membranes between arms, legs and torso.
19 Joints up and down extremities.
20 Quadruped becomes biped or vice versa.

Body parts (d12)

1 Head.
2 Arm.
3 Leg.
4 Torso.
5 Hand.
6 Eye.
7 Mouth.
8 Finger.
9 Teeth.
10 Tongue.
11 Wings/tail or Referee's pick.
12 Referee's pick.

"I Search the Body"

1-50 Number of silver pieces equal to d100 roll just thrown.

51 Hastily-drawn map leading from one place in the Land to another.

52 Flask.

53 Climbing pick.

54 Net.

55–64 10' Rope.

65–76 d6+1 days rations.

RESULTS BELOW should be used once, after that, cross them out and write your own.

76 Letter in a desperate hand (with several cross-outs) explaining how a child was lost in an inexplicable miscarriage.

77 1/4 of a candle-eel (fatty eel that can be used as a candle).

78 Stale piece of bread.

79 Small mirror.

80 Looks similar to healing potions but it's actually a love potion. Drink it and fall in love with whoever last wounded you.

81 Ceremonial silver knife with a specific bishop carved into the pierced blade. Specifically consecrated for an assassination attempt on the bishop by the Cold Banner.

82 Small ivory carved set of shot glasses in the shapes of dead kings.

83 A small vial of **Forgetting Dust**.

84 Recipe for grilled fish in lingonberry sauce.

85 Scrimshaw depiction of battle PCs just fought, clearly recently executed.

86 Deed of sale and map to a large but (seemingly) abandoned castle in a remote corner of the Devoured Land.

87 Contract offering 5,000sp for a living Snow Leopard brought back to Rottingkroner.

88 Sketches, clearly from life, intimately observed and by a talented hand, depicting daughter of a noble house making her way into the Devoured Land.

89 Journal, seemingly written in a calligraphic style characteristic of the monasteries explaining how to read the language of serpents.

90 Exotic black egg, carefully wrapped in a map leading to an icy cliff overlooking a river.

91 Light crossbow w/20 bolts.

92 Bear trap.

93 Sharpened knitting needle (easy to conceal, d4hp).

94 Random Witch Spell scroll.

95 Abortifacient concoction.

96 Change of socks.

97 Piece of cheese.

98 Toy dog carved from wood.

99 Ferret's eye.

00 Ivory belt buckle shaped like a goat.

If You look Closely (d20)

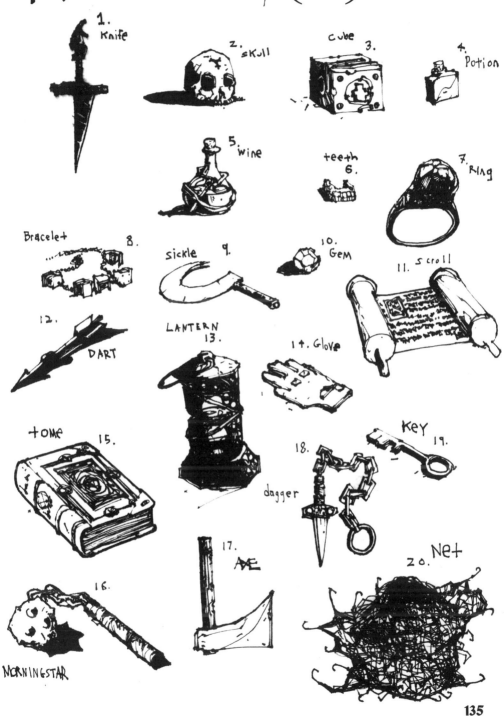

1. Knife
2. skull
3. cube
4. Potion
5. wine
6. teeth
7. Ring
8. Bracelet
9. sickle
10. Gem
11. scroll
12. DART
13. LANTERN
14. Glove
15. tome
16. MORNINGSTAR
17. AXE
18. dagger
19. key
20. Net

Injuries

VIOLENCE IS ALWAYS VIOLENCE but a significant part of expressing the difference between the Devoured Land and the mundane world is the way that violence is described.

The injury tables here are attached to no specific new critical hit mechanic—the basic purpose of the tables is purely verbal: all Referees fall into the trap of describing the same injuries over and over (I know I'm always describing axes going into shoulderblades) and this is meant to lay out the possibilities a little better in the moment. This does not evenly distribute injuries—a body part appears as many times as it has interesting synonyms.

I don't even recommend the Referee roll on them—just keep them handy to look at and let the options seep in while you play. When people die or take massive injuries, pick a kind of trauma and a body part and make a brutal sentence out of it—occasionally throwing in "You pulverize his sternum with your morningstar and cave in his breastbone" instead of "...aaand that soldier's dead" can work wonders.

PICK FROM EACH column, or roll d100 once and read across, or roll once per column

d100	Injury description	Body part description
SLASHING INJURIES		
1	Split	Teeth
2	Slice	Eye
3	Divide	Intestine
4	Cut	Spleen
5	Cleave	Innards
6	Lacerate	Thorax
7	Carve	Thoracic vertebrae
8	Chop	Spinal vertebrae
9	Bisect	Skull
10	Slash	Zygomatic arch
11	Sever	Temporal lobe
12	Rend	Brain
13	Rip	Rib cage
14	Open up	Scapula
15	Shear	Bowels
16	Lop off	Tongue
17	Dice	Spine
18	Mutilate	Spinal cord
19	Remove	Skin
20	Take off	Scalp
21	Sunder	Stomach
22	Hack	Chest
23	Eviscerate	Torso
PIERCING WEAPON INJURIES		
24	Stab	Aorta
25	Lance	Pelvis
26	Jab	Crotch
27	Thrust through	Hipbones
28	Perforate	Jawbone
29	Butcher	Hand
30	Punch through	Carpal bones
31	Run through	Foot
32	Impale	Leg
33	Skewer	Lips
34	Pierce	Arm
35	Poke	Wrist
36	Penetrate	Metacarpals
37	Puncture	Mouth

d100	Injury description	Body part description	d100	Injury description	Body part description
BLUNT WEAPON INJURIES			**FLAME INJURIES, CONTINUED**		
38	Grind	Fingers	69	Boil	Face
39	Mash	Thumb	70	Char	Groin
40	Smash	Coccyx	71	Scorch	Forehead
41	Bash	Gut	72	Set alight	Forearm
42	Mangle	Sternum	73	Toast	Toes
43	Bludgeon	Breastbone	74	Barbecue	Claw
44	Smack	Ribs	75	Broil	Tail(bone)
45	Whack	1st rib, 2nd rib, etc.	76	Cremate	Wing
46	Crack	Liver	77	Roast	Shoulder
47	Pound	Neck	78	Cook	Entrails
48	Break	Kidney	79	Burn	Jaw
49	Shatter	Clavicle	80	Incinerate	Entire body
50	Fracture	Pancreas	81	Singe	Cheek
51	Pulverize	Intestines	82	Melt	Base of the skull
52	Flatten	Lung			
53	Batter	Heart	**GENERAL DESTRUCTION**		
54	Traumatize	Ear	83	Ruin	Head
55	Macerate	Braincase	84	Ravage	Limbs
56	Tenderize	Thigh	85	Eradicate	Paw
57	Pulp	Bicep	86	Wreck	Abdomen
58	Cave in	Deltoid muscle	87	Liquidate	Vertebrae
59	Burst	Ankle	88	Trash	Solar plexus
60	Crush	Nose	89	Collapse	Belly
			90	Liquefy	Between the eyes
BITE INJURIES			91	Undo	Hip
61	Masticate	Elbow	92	Demolish	Breast
62	Eat	Knee	93	Devastate	Ass
63	Gnaw	Kneecap	94	Obliterate	Throat
64	Devour	Upper arm	95	Deconstruct	Collarbone
65	Gnash	Voicebox	96	Cave In	Trunk
66	Bite	Achilles tendon	97	Annihilate	Trachea
67	Swallow	Haunch	98	Destroy	Jugular
68	Chew	Backbone	99	Dismantle	Adam's apple
			00	End	Cranium

Random Encounters

ROLL D100 EVERY 2 hours to see if there's a random encounter and who it is. If you definitely need an encounter during the day, roll d20, if you definitely need an encounter at night, reroll results over 60.

The proper names of animals only necessarily apply the first time a given result is rolled. If, for example, the Referee rolls "Wolves led by Skintaster" a second time, she may opt to have this be another pack altogether.

1   2d4 Frostbitten Moons.

2   d10+10 Frostbitten Moons (or whatever the dominant tribe is in the area).

3   2d6 Maggot Sisters with d4 warpigs.

4   d6 Ulvenbrigad warriors with d4 spellcasters and d6 wolves.

5   2d4 Members of The Thirteen.

6   2d4 Mercenaries of Vryngirslott (Lvl 2 Fighters).

7   d4 Pearlholders.

8   d4+1 members of The Arsonists.

9   Misshaped, carnivorous swan.

10 Avalanche, lake ice breaks, or, if neither are plausible, Misshaped rabbit or other harmless animal.

11 d4 Trolls including Gutterleech, accompanied by d6 Pearlholders.

12 2d6 Wolves, led by Skintaster.

13 d4 Wolves, led by Cromlech.

14 d4+1 Drowning demons.

15 Goat named Facestabber.

16 Werewolf (woman by day, wolf at night).

17 Ratatoskr, the Slandering Marmot.

18 Owl encounter.

19 A random ordinary traveler, probably lost.

20 A frost giant from the Hatemountain.

21–22 Ice Storm--The weather is piercing, impossible, moving forward is hard labor at best. Every PC must roll succeed on a Strength check or movement is impossible for 10 minutes x the number of points the check was failed by. Anyone not in some kind of shelter beyond normal cold-weather gear must save or take 1 hit point of damage for every 10 minutes in the cold.

23 Ice Storm + Encounter—As above plus roll again—something's coming.

24–30 Creatures specifically associated with this hex. If there are none, treat as no encounter.

31 Exertion has made the party hungry, they must eat in the next hour or lose 2hp per hour until they do.

32 Party comes upon a confrontation in progress, roll 2 creatures and then on the "Confrontations" table.

33–48 below apply at NIGHT only—during the day, treat as no encounter

33 Werewolf (in wolf shape).

34 Bjära dragging struggling child to drowning bucket.

35–36 Fox named Gerlioz—if Gerlioz sees the party before it sees her, she will attempt to lead them to another encounter (roll d20 on this table).

38 d4 Serpents, led by Black Tongue.

39 2d4 Snow leopards led by All-Shall-Fall. They seek confusion.

40 d4 Trolls, including Shiverer.

41–42 2d6 Wolves, led by Skintaster.

44–45 2d4 Wolves, led by Cromlech.

46 Cold Banner assassin in disguise as a (roll d4):

   1   Lost traveler.

   2   Member of another Amazon tribe.

   3   Pearlholder.

   4   Someone the party has met before.

47–48 A torch, lantern, or campfire blows out, light another.

49–53 below apply when there are SLEEPING party members only, otherwise treat as no encounter

49 d100 crows, loyal to Vorvik. If any crows escape, 2d6 wolves led by Skintaster will begin discretely tracking the party a half an hour later, attacking when they are weak.

50–51 d4 crows, loyal to Vorvik. If any crows escape, 2d6 wolves led by Skintaster will begin discretely tracking the party a half an hour later, attacking when they are weak.

52–53 Swarm of rats, led by Blasphemer.

54–55 A knot of worms.

56 Snakkur attempts to climb into a PC's mouth.

57 A single crow, seeking to gouge an eye.

58 An owl.

59 Lone witch.

60 Gruntling the troll.

61–72 below apply only in UNCHARTED TERRITORY or when the Referee wishes to introduce a previously hidden landscape feature, otherwise treat as no encounter

61 Dead human.

62 Dead animal.

63 Hut previously hidden by snow, trees or boulders.

64 Forest becomes extra thick or ground becomes rocky and uneven. Movement is halved and encounter checks are doubled (high possibility of ambush).

65 Site of recent battle. 1-3 two groups of humans 4 pair of creatures 5-6 humans vs creatures.

66 Mist-bound valley. Roll Bushcraft to avoid going the wrong way.

67 Remains of a doomed caravan. Various trade goods scattered around.

68 Wolves' den.

69 Old bear traps.

70 Cryptophilic pear, cherry, or plum orchard.

71 Well.

72 A large hollow tree—a blessing to anyone needing shelter but there may be another inhabitant, roll an extra encounter check.

73–00 No encounter.

Rival NPC parties

IF A REFEREE NEEDS to quickly create a party of rival adventurers in the Devoured Land, use the following method. Grab *one of each kind of die* and roll them all.

D4-1 The number of **horses** and/or **dogs** the party has brought

D6 Number of **Fighters**

D8 Average party **level**

D10 Motive

1 Aimless treasure hunting.
2 Escorting a pregnant patron in search of Amazons willing to help terminate the pregnancy.
3 Bounty hunters looking for a fugitive.
4 Fugitives hiding from the law.
5 Seeking a specific storied magic item.
6 Seeking to rob Amazon tribes.
7 Scientific/geographic expedition.
8 Tracking a lost merchant caravan.
9 Hunting a werewolf or other creature to its lair.
10 Lost.

D12 Additional members

1 Magic-User
2 Specialist
3 Cleric
4-7 Two Specialists
8 Two Magic-Users
9-10 Magic-User and Specialist
11 Cleric, Magic-User, Specialist
12 Two specialists, Magic-User

D20 Quirk

1 True reason for expedition is known only to leader (roll another d20).
2 They have a useful magic item.
3 One wants to collect a bounty on one of the PCs for some crime.
4 Will attempt to befriend and then betray PCs.
5 Internal divisions: one half of the party plots against the other.
6 They are hallucinating wildly after a run-in with The Thirteen.
7 They have recently escaped some Amazons and are at half hp.
8 d4 of them are werewolves.
9 They are infected with Worm Rot.
10 They have a snow leopard in a cage they hope to return to civilization for a reward.
11 They carry gems worth their weight in silver.
12 They carry a box which contains a demon.
13 They are out of food.
14 They have d6 random Witch spells on scrolls.
15 One member believes they carry a demon child and they hope to have it aborted.
16 They are all female and hope to join the Amazons.
17 They are being harried by a group of Pearlholders that outnumbers them by d4.
18 They have a map to the Dim Fortress.
19 One is a disguised member of the Cold Banner.
20 They carry crates of trade goods that're worth 3500sp if they can be taken back to civilization.

ASSUME NPC SPECIALISTS in these circumstances have x3 Sneak Attack and d8-3 extra skill points in any other skill they might need as it comes up (up to the maximum for their level), Magic-Users have *Sleep* and a 1 in 4 chance of having any other spell that they might need when it comes up (up to the maximum for their level), and Clerics have *Cure Light Wounds* plus a 50% chance of having any other spell they might need when it comes up (up to the maximum for their level).

index

END.

Tumbledown inn overrun by wharf rats in search of **Ribboned Jenny**, a fancy-rat from **Rottingkroner** (see H5).

Note: each area measures 6 miles across, regardless of shape on the map.

A small case in red frogskin lying in the dirt harbors a love potion and a candle whose light exposes fae, false, invisible and magical things.

Shifting winds have revealed a princess voluntarily encased in ice for one thousand three hundred years. On her twentieth birthday, court seers had informed the unkillable girl that she was cursed to slay the next person she laid eyes upon—and she decided she would rather not. If freed, she'll immediately take her leave but improbably cross paths with her liberator with Jennifer-Aniston-movie-esque frequency forever thereafter. Actually, she isn't going to kill anyone—the prophecy was just wrong. It turns out the entrails for "repeatedly run through" and "repeatedly run into" are gratingly similar.

A pack **goat** named Sprogsmal trundles across the plain, its mistress, a poet, long dead. Its saddlebags contain poems worth 3000sp to anyone with a large purse and a respect for quality literature.

Fourteen children ages 6-12. Armed and averse to adult supervision. They'll probably be eaten soon. One has a random **Witch Spell** on a scroll which she will read if threatened.

Cave walls dense with nested and discoesque cubes of pyrite reflect not the present but the future selves of the PCs. Two encounter checks worth of study will reveal enough details of accessory and scar to grant insight into future dangers and opportunities—the observer is +2 to saves until the next level-up—or the Referee may offer the player a fortune from the table in *Vornheim: The Complete City Kit* should he or she have access to that remarkable and indispensable tome.

A murder of **crows** under **Black Sky** scavenge a wolf kill in a shallow valley—a luckless neophyte of the Maggot Sisterhood. They snatch at both her jewelry (150sp worth) and the branded skin beneath.

The main force of the Amazons of the **Ulvenbrigad** is here, in hilltop earthworks that twist like an intestinal tract, overlooking the "trap town" of Thridi. **Chiord**, the sacred bastard, wallows feverishly in a rockpiled redoubt at the center of the hill and the approaches are thick with scarred sentinels and guard **wolves**.

Mauthlic Gaunt is, one hopes, some kind of anthropologist. At any rate, he has a trunk full of dolls and effigies gathered from across the continent. If the party tells him about the snow man in Eelhome, he will pay them 1000sp to take him safely to it, and will reward them with 1000sp more upon arrival out of sheer joy.

A party member will feel their foot snap through a membrane stretched like drumleather just beneath the snow's surface. This turns out to be the wing of a vast pale dead ancient winged reptile the size of a god, stretched between bones thick as ash trunks. A Magic-User examining this skin for two weeks will gain a level—providing they can read the language of **serpent** skins.

A hilltop ring of simple graves like outsize molars, interlaced with mutilated **Ulvenbrigad** slain in an ambush by the **Frostbitten Moons**. One has the *Whispering Panic* spell stabbily tattooed on her left arm.

The Spitter is a foreign scholar monk who sits contemplating the mountains and the nature of truth. Using medieval standards for both, pick a distant land and a sexual impropriety. He hails from the first and has been exiled for the second. The Spitter is fond of hiking, eager to trade information and sworn to eschew violence. He is evil if you like.

Low slanting walls of larvikite slab form the home of Pleasant Lora the alewidow, who brews a storied bock. Rare visitors have bartered a wide enough variety of durable goods in exchange for lager that her home is now about as close as the western Devoured gets to a trading post. Her hearth is warm and her inventory is fairly random.

A large and unusually cryophilic plum tree is home to **Ratatoskr**, the Slandering Marmot.

Lord Amozark (Lvl 6 Fighter) and three lieutenant constables have tracked the **Arsonists** (in Area 2F) to the Devoured Land from **Rottingkroner**. He is attempting to bring them in for the murder of one Aarstein Oyseth and will mistake the players' characters for the patchwork band of heavily-armed eccentrics he seeks.

The small, remote settlement known as Thridi has light in the windows and hogs in the pens. These lie—Thridi was raided months ago by the **Ulvenbrigad**, and this show of shelter and warmth is used to entrap ignorant animals and travelers to relieve them of their meat and valuables, respectively.

A surveyor lies dead. **Worms** crawl into him and then out again. His notebook contains a sketch of the location of the tower of the **Cold Banner** (unlabeled) (see E1), a drawing of a skeleton in a moldy jerkin, and the names of 2 **drowning demons**.

Pearlholders have nailed a pair of lovers to either side of a yew, inverted, with three large nails outside one of their churches. One stake through their trunks and the tree's, two more through the backs of their hands, nailed knuckle to knuckle. One woman is dead, the other will be soon. Her dying wish is vengeance. Their crime was never explained.

A bridge above the lair of two **trolls**, **Gruntling** and The Fibbing Troll, provides the only access to the oozing volcanic caldera of Lachrymose Peak. Manheim the clown (see E8) is among the many luckless souls still alive in the Troll's Effigy Net. There is also a scroll with a random **Witch Spell** on one of the dead victims.

A tongue of ice, 200' tall and 5' wide tumbles from one distributary of the Slith down into another. Climbing this frozen waterfall offers a secret entrance to the trolls' lair at **Lachrymose Peak**. From the Days of the Threshold (April) until the Days of the Rainsnout (November) the route thaws and this route is inaccessible.

The large black sessile oaks that twist their way across the town and upper altitudes are particularly thick here. An encounter roll of 21-30 indicates an ambush by creatures of the Referee's choice.

This wood is the territory of **Transcending Massacre** and her drift of 16 snow leopards.

The witch called **Thorn** passes through the wood riding her wolf, **Lair Abbess** on her way to meet her sisters in G8. She will be offended if fellow travelers refuse her gifts of lutefisk and doghead pie, which are, of course, poisoned and will turn them into lemmings.

Like a rusted-out collander, skeletal black against the sky, an ancient gallows-dome occupies a flattened peak. There are only two bodies hung from the vaulting woodwork, a useless crab pudding, and the author of a despicable surgeon, installed here by the **Ulvenbrigad** in an extending web of their own entrails through which small animals creep to feast on their remains.

Mammoth skulls and the smell of butchered geese announce the southernmost rim of the territory of the **Frostbitten Moons**. These **Amazons** dwell in the dead batteries and outworks of a lost castle or fortified city. Approaching from leeward, the party will see the leaning and snow-covered ruin-homes striped in bright yellow with luminous paint.

Mist like clotted milk. A failed (passive) Bushcraft roll brings the party out in an adjacent area other than the one they intended.

Two old men walk along a bridge of whitewood and bog iron bisecting the Slith. Neither knows the other is a disguised immortal. They are Onthryn Star-Eater, Lord of botulism and whales and Vystrid Innyrthronde, Maker of all Claws. They discuss politics and the sea.

A parliament of **owls** nests here, ruled by **Stryx**. Their vocabulary is growing. If the party has already had an owl encounter but has not summoned them, they will only hear them hooting.

Prince Nygnengeth of **Nornrik** and eight huntsmen seek the Narthex Hart, a legendary stag whose antlers respectively map and reflect the route of the Slith and its river system. It does not exist. They are Fighters of whatever level you prefer.

Speaking of massacres, this area of the wood contains the home of a lone girl whose family has been slain by leopards or wolves. There is a beetle in the bath and no chairs.

On the edge of the forest lies the **Sevenfold Tower**, containing seven temptations, seven curses and seven treasures.

A small black ceramic jar in an abandoned watermill contains a vial of poison and a scroll inscribed with the *Chain of Skin* spell.